Jewish Wisdom for Business Success

JEWISH WISDOM FOR BUSINESS SUCCESS

LESSONS FROM THE TORAH AND OTHER ANCIENT TEXTS

RABBI LEVI BRACKMAN

AND

SAM JAFFE

AMACOM

AMERICAN MANAGEMENT ASSOCIATION

New York · Atlanta · Brussels · Chicago · Mexico City · San Francisco
Shanghai · Tokyo · Toronto · Washington, D.C.

Special discounts on bulk quantities of AMACOM books are available to corporations, professional associations, and other organizations. For details, contact Special Sales Department, AMACOM, a division of American Management Association, 1601 Broadway, New York, NY 10019.
Tel.: 212-903-8316.   Fax: 212-903-8083.
Website: www.amacombooks.org/go/specialsales

This publication is designed to provide accurate and authoritative information in regard to the subject matter covered. It is sold with the understanding that the publisher is not engaged in rendering legal, accounting, or other professional service. If legal advice or other expert assistance is required, the services of a competent professional person should be sought.

Library of Congress Cataloging-in-Publication Data

Brackman, Levi.
  Jewish wisdom for business success : lessons from the Torah and other ancient texts / Rabbi Levi Brackman and Sam Jaffe.
      p.   cm.
  Includes bibliographical references and index.
  ISBN-13: 978-0-8144-1274-9
  ISBN-10: 0-8144-1274-2
    1. Success in business—Religious aspects.   2. Entrepreneurship—Religious aspects.   3. Economics—Religious aspects—Judaism.   I. Jaffe, Sam.   II. Title.

  HF5386.B735   2008
  296.3'83—dc22

                                                2008010370

Printing number

10   9   8   7   6   5   4   3   2   1

In honor of Torah scholars throughout the ages

CONTENTS

INTRODUCTION

Why have so many Jews been successful at business? There are plenty of theories: genetics, cultural sensibilities, the herring. We don't agree with any of them. But before we present our answer to the question, here's the story on which the herring theory is based:

> A Jewish peddler was taking a train from Minsk to Pinsk. Stuffed with his wares into a tiny cabin with several other people, goats, and chickens, he was surprised to see an officer of the Czar's army enter through the door. "The first class cabins are full," said the officer, a look of disgust spreading across his face as he realized who his traveling companions would be for the long ride.
>
> The Jewish fellow, paying respect to one of his country's warriors, stood up from his seat and motioned for the officer to sit down in his place. The officer, pleased, took the seat and eyed his benefactor curiously. "Are you Jewish?" he asked.
>
> "Last time I checked I was," the peddler said, nervously fingering the knots of his prayer garment.
>
> "Tell me," said the officer, a light growing in his eyes, "why are you Jews so good at business? You seem like a nice chap. Tell me what your people's secret is."

The peddler narrowed his eyes, as if thinking hard. "I'm sorry, but I can't," he said. "I've been sworn to secrecy."

"I'll give you ten rubles," the officer said excitedly. "I've got to know."

"Ten rubles? What secret is worth 10 rubles? I've sold shmattes for more than ten rubles, but I've given an oath! Ten rubles is not worth my sworn oath."

"Okay. I'll give you 100 rubles." The officer pulled out a crisp 100 ruble note and held it in front of the peddler. The man leaned over the seated officer and whispered something into his ear while deftly relieving his hand of the 100 ruble note at the same time. He stood straight up and looked out the window, ignoring the officer's puzzled expression.

"Schmaltz herring?" the officer asked.

"That's what we eat. Start eating a lot of it, all the time. Pretty soon, you'll notice that your business acumen is improving. Over time, you'll find yourself raking in the rubles." The train pulled into the station and the peddler tipped his hat and made his way out of the cabin. "Ah, here's Pinsk. Good luck with the schmaltz herring, sir, and please don't tell anyone that it was me that let out the secret."

A few months later, the peddler was manning his clothing stand near the Pinsk railway station when he heard the din of galloping hoofbeats behind him. He turned around to see the officer, fury in his eyes, reining in his horse. "I finally found you, you scoundrel," bellowed the officer. "I want my money back!" He dismounted. In his hand was a glass jar of schmaltz herring.

"I've been eating this stuff for breakfast, lunch, and dinner. It's awful! It tastes like grease mixed with dirt. You fooled me once, but you won't fool me again . . ."

"I don't understand, sir," the peddler said. "What is wrong?"

"What's wrong? I gave you a hundred rubles and you told me to eat schmaltz herring and it would make me a smart businessman. Now I realize that you've tricked me . . ." The officer stopped in mid-breath, amazed that instead of cowering in fear, the peddler was smiling and nodding his head knowingly.

"Good," said the peddler, smiling. "I see the schmaltz herring is working."

But for those of you—like us—who are not convinced of the herring theory, let's ask the question again. Why have so many Jews been successful at making money? The truth is that it's a question which many people mull silently, but few dare to ask openly. Fears of being labeled an anti-Semite—or worse, causing others to indulge in anti-Semitism—are the main reasons for the collective avoidance of this topic.

But that doesn't mean that it's not a legitimate question. After all, Jews make up less than two-tenths of a percentage point of the world's population—yes, only .02 percent—yet they represent more than 10 percent of the Forbes 400 list of the world's wealthiest people, more than 10 percent of the Fortune list of the CEOs of the 500 largest corporations in the world, and almost 30 percent of all the Nobel Prize winners. Jews are disproportionately represented in many high-income fields, such as medicine, law, and finance. Jews do seem to have some sort of advantage when it comes to financial success.

In the early part of the last century—the first extended period of time when Jews were allowed to participate in the social, financial, and cultural realms of the larger society in Europe and America—many people struggled with this question. Unfortunately, they too often made the error of assuming that Jews were so successful because they cheated. In the United States, Henry Ford self-published a book about "the Jewish problem," entitled *The International Jew: The World's Foremost Problem,* which urged his fellow citizens to stand in the way of this foreign race that was becoming too successful too quickly. Ford's writings turned out to be the rants of a doddering old fool. But in Germany, Adolf Hitler published a similar book, *Mein Kampf,* and the world burned for more than a decade as a result.

So the puzzle over the question of Jewish success in business has stayed in a box in the corner of intellectual discussion, unopened out of fear of repeating historical mistakes.

As the authors of this book, we disagree with the view that says the box should remain closed. We feel that we know the answer to the question. And our hypothesis might be even more controversial than the act of raising the topic. It's not the schmaltz herring, an international cabal, or genetics. We believe that the root cause of Jewish success in business lays in the book Jews hold most dear and sacred—the Torah.

"Being Jewish" means different things to different people. To some, it's about a political movement—Zionism. To others, it's about a specific culture, complete with its own accent, ethics, and sense of humor. To yet others, it's simply a type of cuisine. But the one thing that everyone agrees about is that Judaism is a religion, a religion guided by a book called the Torah, also known as the Hebrew Bible (and to Christians as the Old Testament).

Although not all Jews are religious and many do not have a scholarly grasp of the Torah, they all still carry on a nearly four-thousand-year-old tradition. Some claim it's a genetic inheritance. Others might call it a form of a Jungian collective unconscious. We call it osmosis. For millennia, the Torah and its stories, traditional explanations, and values were taught intensively to every Jew from childhood to old age. Although some Jews abandoned the active study of the Torah in the last two centuries, they still grew up in a society permeated with knowledge of Torah and its unique view of the world. Even a Jew born in the baby boom after World War II, who can't remember any relatives who studied Torah every day and lived by its commandments, still has something very real in common with all other Jews. It's a particular sense of right and wrong, a unique ordering of priorities, and a way of doing things that reaches back to founding fathers like Moses and Abraham and founding mothers like Leah and Rachel.

At this point, we may have left some of our non-Jewish readers mystified. Religion, they may say, is about revelation, prophets, and divinity. How can you propose a theory which says that sacred religious writings are the source of business success?

People who are familiar with the Jewish religion and its impact on a person's daily life will be much more understanding of our suggestion. Judaism, after all, is a religion primarily of the here and now. The observant Jew follows rules that originated from the Torah, rules that govern, among other things, how to get out of bed, how to dress, how to wash your hands, how to eat, how to pray, how to parent your children, how to respect your elders, how to observe a lightning storm. . . . The list could go on for pages. And we're not talking about customs. All these activities have rules. Rules that were formulated over three and a half thousand years ago. Rules that are still being observed by some adherents of the religion.

For such an all-encompassing religion, it is not surprising that the Torah has opinions on how to make money. That is, after all, what human beings have spent the majority of their waking hours doing for at least the last five thousand years. To say that the Torah just ignores that facet of our lives would be a hard bone to swallow.

But our hypothesis is even bolder than some might expect. We aren't just saying that the Torah speaks about business ethics (it does that also)—it goes much deeper. The Torah offers a blueprint for the businessperson to create, maintain, and grow a profitable and successful enterprise. That blueprint isn't in PowerPoint format or sketched on a whiteboard in some synagogue office. It's hidden deep within the Hebrew Bible and its auxiliary texts known together as the Torah. The etymology of word Torah is *hora-ah*, which means "to teach," and the book you are currently reading takes the teachings and lessons of the Torah and shows how they relate to business success.

A word about how we define the texts of the Torah. Jews have always seen the Torah as having two texts that depend on each other and are thus inseparable. The two components of the Torah are the written law and the oral law. The written law, which the rest of the world refers to as the Old Testament, comprises the five books of Moses, the Prophets, and the Scriptures. The oral law is comprised of the Talmud, the Midrash, and the Kabbalah. The "oral law" is termed as such because, like many other bodies of work in the ancient world before the invention of the printing press, it was originally transmitted orally. It was eventually written down by the rabbis who worried that it would otherwise be lost; thus, the oral law now consists of written texts. According to tradition, both the written and the oral law were handed to Moses from God on Mount Sinai approximately thirty-five hundred years ago.

Interwoven within Torah writings about other aspects of life and religious principles are lessons that a businessperson can use to become successful. But nowhere has this business advice been compiled and summarized—until now.

This book is an attempt at just such a compendium. We have taken ideas from Torah texts and woven them around the theme of success in business. But we aren't the original authors of this text. Our only feat is in compiling and commenting upon the Torah works of the scholars who have come before us.

Many of the chapters are built around a story from the Torah that has been expanded and interpreted in the Talmud or Midrash. We also delve into the Zohar and other mystical texts of the Kabbalah (the Torah's mystical writings). We write about the teachings of some of the Hasidic masters as well, some of whom had plenty to say about business practices. And we haven't forgotten to add insights from modern-day rabbinical giants, chief among them the Lubavitcher Rebbe Menachem Mendel Schneerson, who found time amidst his Torah studies and writings to counsel many successful businessmen before he passed away in 1994.

While we view this book as an extension of those earlier scholars, we have done something unique that is not a tradition in Torah literature: we've woven in modern-day examples of real events and anecdotes that echo the themes about which we write. Some of these anecdotes are based on interviews we've done with successful businesspeople. Others are based on press reports and autobiographies. They all illustrate the concept being discussed in that section of the book, but they do so from the real world of business, not from the writing table of a rabbi. The purpose of the real-life anecdotes is to show how the Torah writings, however old they may be, are still relevant today.

We also close each chapter subsection with two summations of the message contained therein. The first compiles the specific insight for business practices, which that section has discussed. And since our character and personal life has a direct impact on our success in business, we have also added a second insight that sheds light on how the ideas may be applied to our personal lives.

Finally, we end each chapter with a meditation exercise that you can use if you're so inclined. Meditation (in Hebrew, it's called *hitbonenut*) is an important, if recently ignored, part of the Jewish tradition. In the Appendix, we include a guide to Jewish meditation that you should read before trying any of the meditation exercises. If you would like to further explore subjects covered in this book or meet people who are discussing them, please feel free to visit www.levibrackman.com.

We hope that the wisdom and insights of Torah and its tradition of many generations shine through this book. We are certain that all readers, of all religions and backgrounds, can learn something about elevating the world of business and even the act of making money, into the realm of the sacred. Above all, we wish you much success in all your business endeavors, and that with the help of this book you will surely be able to achieve real and sustained financial success.

ACKNOWLEDGMENTS

First and foremost, my gratitude and thanks goes to Almighty God Creator of us all, for giving me the privilege of immersing myself in the study of Torah from childhood onwards. I have benefited immensely from the insight and wisdom of the Torah, and I am enormously grateful for having been given that opportunity.

Sheindy, my wife, is a constant inspiration and source of encouragement. Sheindy, your belief in me is only rivaled by my love for you—it is a privilege to be walking down life's path together with you.

I have been blessed to have had many wonderful teachers who had major impacts on me and whose influence is therefore felt in this book. Two of them I would particularly like to thank here. Rabbi Moshe Stern, of my alma mater The Rabbinical College of Canada, really opened my eyes to the vastness and beauty of Talmudic study and taught me how to plumb its depths. My appreciation also goes to Rabbi Melech Zwible, of my other alma mater, the Rabbinical College of America, who gave me a profound appreciation of the study of the Kabbalah and taught me how to incorporate its teachings into my life.

My brother-in-law and friend Yisroel (Matthew) Nyman read the entire manuscript and made invaluable comments and suggestions and the book is better off for his input. I would also like to thank my dear friend Lou Kravitz for reviewing most of the manuscript and making valuable comments—Lou, your support and friendship is appreciated beyond words. Thanks also go to my buddy Scott Patten for reviewing and commenting on the chapter on negotiating.

This book could not have been written without the cooperation of many senior businesspeople who gave time from their busy schedule to talk about the ideas found in the book. For this I offer my personal gratitude to David Einhorn of Greenlight Capital, Lou Hoffman of the Hoffman Agency, Howard Jonas of IDT, Keith Pritchard of Navone Investments, and Sheryl Sandberg, formerly of Google, now of Facebook.

Similarly, I would also like to express gratitude to my friends Jonathan Beren of Z Commercial Properties, David Drucker of At Contact, Even Makovsky of Shames-Makovsky Realty, Larry Mizel of MDC Holdings, David Slager of Atticus Capital, and Jim Williams of Southwestern Production—your advice toward the making of this book is reflected in it and is greatly appreciated, as is your support of my organizations Judaism in the Foothills and The Movement for a Tolerant World.

Sam Jaffe is my coauthor and friend. When Sam first suggested I write a book about Judaism's advice for business success, I told him that I would only do it if he coauthored it with me. As they say, the rest is history. Sam, I appreciate your partnership in this endeavor. I would also like to thank Sam's talented wife, Myung Oak Kim, for reviewing and making comments on the entire manuscript.

My literary agent and friend Gary Heidt believed in me as a writer from day one, even before I had a viable book project that he could sell. I thank him for that. Thank you Bob Nirkind, senior editor at AMACOM, for your input and faith in this project. Thanks to Debbie Posner, who copyedited the entire manuscript and in doing so made it more readable and lucid. I would also like to thank Mike Sivilli, associate editor at AMACOM, for his devotion throughout the editing process. Appreciation also goes to Jeremiah Birnbaum for doing an outstanding job in proofreading the book.

My Mom, Mrs. Sarah Feldman, has spent countless hours editing and critiquing my writing, and has made me a substantially better writer. For that and much more, I thank her profusely.

I would also like to acknowledge my wonderful little boys Dovi, Benny, and Shmuley, who remind me each day of the abundant blessing that is life itself.

Finally, deep thanks and appreciation go to my late father and mentor Dr. Derek Brackman, who taught me the importance of critical thinking, hard work, and the joy of following my authentic desire—values and teachings which imbue the pages of this book.

Rabbi Levi Brackman

Jewish Wisdom for Business Success

CHAPTER 1

JOURNEY FORTH!

Conquering Fear

The whole world is a narrow bridge. The important thing is to have no fear.

—HASIDIC MASTER RABBI NACHMAN OF BRESLOV

ON A HUMID SUMMER'S DAY IN CALIFORNIA DURING 2003, SHERYL Sandberg was experiencing fear. She was about to walk into her boss's office and tell him that the project she was overseeing was out of control.

Sandberg's career had begun in Washington, D.C., where she worked as chief of staff to Treasury Secretary Lawrence Summers during the Clinton administration. When Clinton left office in 2001, she decided to try her hand at business and moved to Silicon Valley.

She signed on with Sergey Brin and Larry Page, who had recently taken leave from their graduate studies at Stanford University. At the time, they were trying to turn their start-up into a player in the search engine industry. That company—Google—would go on to become one of the most astounding successes in global corporate history. At that time, however, it was just another struggling start-up and Sandberg was one of its earliest employees.

But on that day in 2003, Sandberg had to report on a project that had gone awry. In her attempt to manage the project to success, she had taken on too much risk and it was now losing money.

She could have tried to cover up the mistake, insisting that the project was going well and she just needed more time and money. Or she could have tried to blame another executive who had been remotely involved in the project. Instead, as she entered the executive suite, she chose a third path. She told Brin and Page: "I screwed up. I lost the company money."

Page's response shocked her. "He told me that the biggest mistake is to go too slow, not too fast," Sandberg recalled. "The company would never get anywhere if we spent our time avoiding mistakes out of a fear of failure. He congratulated me and then sent me on my way."

Sandberg, as the vice president of global sales, went on to spearhead Google's advertising projects, including the rollout of its AdWords program, which links paid advertisements to search results. It has allowed Google to turn their search engine from a cool tool into an extremely profitable business. Sandberg says that she never could have realized the success of the AdWords project if she had been paralyzed by the fear of making a mistake. Early in 2008, she left Google to become the second-in-command of Facebook, the emerging social-networking company.

The other major search engines—Yahoo, AOL, and Microsoft— had ignored Google in its early years. They were comfortable with their own business model, which charged money to Websites in order to give them a higher ranking in the search results. They knew that using Google's software would give browsers a superior search, but it also would eliminate a stream of revenue. The fear of losing that revenue stream drove each one of them to reject Google's early offers to power their search engines with its software.

So Google went forward alone and fashioned its own brand. By the time 75 percent of Web users were choosing Google to execute their searches, it was too late for Yahoo, AOL, and Microsoft to partner with the start-up. Google had already won the race.

Fear, as Sandberg learned that day, can be the single-biggest obstacle a person faces when trying to accomplish a goal. Unfortunately, it seems that modern society has developed into a fear-worshipping machine. Fear, more than any other emotion, is what drives many people to do what they do. And most of that fear is irrational.

If Internet titans like Yahoo, AOL, and Microsoft can be so paralyzed by fear that they don't act even when it is in their own interest to do so, imagine how much it pervades the thoughts of businesspeople in more established and conservative industries. When companies have hindsight and look back at their mistakes, the core of the problem can often be traced to fear.

The Four Faces of Fear

Many successful businesspeople will tell you that they were able to achieve success after conquering their inner fears. From that point on, the road to success was a relatively straight shot.

Every religion and school of philosophy views fear as an obstacle and urges followers to struggle against it. The Torah goes one step further. Hidden deep within it is a blueprint for overcoming negative fear-based reactions. It's based on the well-known story of Moses and the splitting of the sea. This blueprint for defeating fear is found in the text of the Torah and in the additional stories and teachings about events mentioned in the Torah, known as midrashim (the plural of "midrash"). Midrashim were handed down orally from generation to generation, and only written down many centuries later. Typically, a midrash is a sophisticated commentary that sheds light on one of the deeper issues raised by a passage from the Torah.

In this case, the midrash (Michilta, Exodus 14:12) takes the form of a story about the argument among the newly emancipated Israelites as they stood before the Sea of Reeds (which is often mistakenly translated in English versions of the Torah as the Red Sea). They were caught between the chasing Egyptian soldiers and the deep waters. As you can imagine, they were very afraid (Exodus 14).

Fear, in fact, drove them towards recommending four modes of action that would have been disastrous. The midrash goes on to discuss these four faces of fear: self-sabotage, fight, retreat, and learned helplessness. Moses's response, found in the Torah, shows timeless wisdom for overcoming these four impulses. He doesn't just anticipate Nike's advertising slogan and tell the Israelites to "Just Do It!" He accepts the source of their fear and tells them how to overcome it. In doing so, he creates a template that anyone can use in any situation where fear is present. That template is so effective that it needs no updating—even three-and-a-half thousand years after Moses created it.

Moses's stand took place at the sandy shoreline of the Sea of Reeds in the Sinai Peninsula, which is about as far as you can get from Silicon Valley. But the lessons taught by Moses are as relevant today as they were then. The Israelites had just been released from slavery and were allowed to flee toward their homeland. But Pharaoh changed his mind. He called his cavalry and led them across the desert to catch up with his former slaves.

Imagine what it was like to be one of the Israelites gathered at the water's edge, with the hoofbeats of Pharaoh's cavalry booming in the near distance. The exultation of freedom is gone. You glance in one direction at the endless water and in the other direction at the looming war horses. You can hear the war-whoops of the charioteers. You look upwards at the sky, wishing you had wings, and wonder to yourself whether this is your last chance to gaze at the clouds drifting in the sky. The dust from the approaching army starts to cloud the air around you. You look into the eyes of your children and you feel their fear in your own bones.

Here is where the midrash adds some pertinent details. At this profoundly terrifying moment, it tells us that the leaders of the people split into four camps, arguing furiously with each other.

One elder is calling for the people to commit mass suicide. "It is better to die by one's own hand than to be murdered by our former masters. It would be one last statement of free will and self control: To prove we are no longer slaves, we must lift our knives to our throats by our own accord!"

A second man shouts him down. "The moment of freedom is gone," he says wearily. "Let us prostrate ourselves before Pharaoh again and return to Egypt as slaves. That is all we ever were and that is what we should remain."

The spokesman for another group becomes agitated and raises his voice in fury. "Free men must fight for their freedom," he cries. "Now is the time to rise up and do battle with the Egyptians. No matter how poorly armed we are and how inevitable the outcome of such a battle must be, let us fight back."

A final voice interrupts his speech. "We did not free ourselves from slavery. We've never been in control. Our only path is to remain motionless, close our eyes, and pray to God."

Pharaoh's lead horse was now clearly visible and the sun glinted off his raised sword. The people fell silent and looked to Moses. He had guided them this far. Moses looked out upon his people and uttered perhaps the most important words he would ever speak as a leader (Exodus 14:13–14): "Do not fear. Stand firm and see the salvation which God will bring today. Though you see the Egyptians now, you will never see them again. God will fight for you and you shall remain silent."

The people stood, speechless, puzzled by Moses's words. Then God spoke to Moses and told him to give the Israelites one last command (Exodus 15:1): "Now journey forth!"

Journey forth? To where? To walk towards the onslaught of the Egyptians would be journeying backwards, so that could not be what he means. The only other place to go would be into the deep water. That would surely lead to a horrible death by drowning.

The awful paralysis that overtook the Israelites at that moment is what many of us feel in our work lives. The motivations for that fear are also the same as the four faces of fear the Israelites vocalized that day. The following sections will discuss them in greater detail.

INSIGHT FOR BUSINESS: *Competition is not your real enemy—fear is. Choosing to follow the path of safety will cost you opportunities that will often be far greater than the potential losses you might incur by a riskier path.*

INSIGHT FOR LIFE: *The payoff for avoiding mistakes is often smaller than what you may gain from taking risks. Allow yourself to take risks. Remember, it's better to be an imperfect achiever than to avoid the journey altogether.*

Self-Sabotage

Torah commentaries see each of Moses's abovementioned four statements—1. Do not fear; 2. Stand firm and see the salvation which God will bring today; 3. Though you see the Egyptians now, you will never see them again; and 4. God will fight for you and you shall remain silent—as individual responses to each of the fear-based arguments that had been voiced to him.

The first camp, remember, called for a mass suicide. While they might have felt some measure of self-respect by choosing their own fate, this option was clearly a path to nowhere. The goal of leaving Egypt wasn't to prove some intellectual point. It was to return home as free men. Killing themselves offered no hope of accomplishing that goal.

It is not surprising, though, that some Israelites argued for this path. Suicide is just another form of self-sabotage. People often choose to quit because they fear that they might fail. Often they decide to opt out of things because they are afraid of being forced to do so by others. Self-sabotage is caused by fear of rejection or failure. This happens as much in business at it does in other parts of our lives, such as relationships and athletics.

Hence Moses's admonishment to the people arguing for this course: "Do not fear!" This was not just a command; it also was a profound piece of advice. Moses was telling his people that they must acknowledge that their fear was driving them towards suicide and self-sabotage. Before you can fight the urge to self-destruct, you must acknowledge the source of the defeatist attitude, and that is fear. Once you admit that fear is what is really driving you, you will recognize that all the arguments to sustain the conclusion of defeat and sabotage are flawed. Then you realize that other avenues are available, and suicide or defeat vanishes as an option.

TARGETED GENETICS: A COMPANY THAT CHOSE TO LIVE

While it's not possible for a business to physically commit suicide, there have certainly been cases where executives chose complete surrender. There have also been instances where executives have hung on at any cost—and were happy that they did.

One such company is a small Seattle biotechnology start-up called Targeted Genetics. Founded in 1996, its mission was to take promising research in the field of gene therapy and turn it into a profitable business (and cure a few diseases along the way).

The problem was that gene therapy was a new technology and the public demanded—rightfully so—that it be tested exhaustively before its widespread use. The entire gene therapy industry had nearly ground to a halt in 1999, when a clinical trial volunteer died after being given an overdose of the medication being tested (not, by the way, a Targeted Genetics drug). Investors fled the field and companies shifted their focus to other technologies.

But Targeted Genetics was founded on the premise of gene therapy. Abandoning it would destroy the company's original mission, and money was running out. By 2001, the company was down to a few million dollars in cash. Shutting its doors became a real possibility.

But the company's CEO, H. Stewart Parker, refused to surrender. She dismissed more than two-thirds of the staff and reduced the number of compounds the company was trying to develop. She also vigorously scouted for partnerships with larger, better capitalized biotech companies.

By May of 2008, Targeted Genetics was still developing its two primary drug candidates, but it no longer had significant cash flow problems. Thanks to successful partnerships and new stock issuances, the company had built up its cash position to more than $12 million. More importantly, its biggest potential product, an AIDS vaccine, was ready to enter an enormous trial in Africa and Asia that could make it the first preventative medication for the virus. Although the trial may still fail, it is closer to fruition than any other AIDS vaccine. If it succeeds, the vaccine will be available to newborns in the developing world, ensuring that the newest generation will not suffer through that terrible disease. Targeted Genetics never would have reached this point if the company had surrendered completely in 2001.

Thus, although it is often attractive to give up when the going gets tough, it is fear that often drives us to make that wrong choice. Moses was able to see beyond the present and into tomorrow; he saw that if the Israelites marched forward, miraculous things could happen—and they did happen. The sea opened for them to cross. He beseeched the Israelites to acknowledge their fear, for then they would be better equipped to overcome it. This is what H. Stewart Parker saw as well. Like most successful businesspeople, defeat was not an option for Moses. However bad things may seem today, there is always a brighter tomorrow to work toward.

> **INSIGHT FOR BUSINESS:** *There are cases where complete surrender is the right thing. They are, however, extremely rare. If it seems like a compelling choice, get as much feedback from others to determine if your judgment is based in financial reality, or if it has become clouded by fear.*

> **INSIGHT FOR LIFE:** *We all have a tendency to indulge in self-sabotage—failure can sometimes seem a welcome relief from the pain of staying in the game. Always fight that urge. Self-sabotage is just another form of servitude. And be aware that suicide is the ultimate self-sabotage.*

Fight

So now back to the Israelites and the wisdom of Moses. To the second group of Israelites—those crying out for battle—Moses says: "Stand firm and see the salvation that God will bring about today." Again, the meaning in the words themselves is a bit cloudy. But when put in the context of a response to an ill-conceived call to arms, the wisdom becomes clearer.

When we are particularly fearful of an adversary, fighting back is often the most satisfying option. The desire to battle the Egyptians is an understandable and even commendable reaction to the fear the Israelites felt towards them. But it takes an enormous reserve of energy to fight. Resources are stretched and often wasted.

Additionally, to fight the Egyptians, the Israelites would have had to turn and aim their attention backwards. The goal was to get home, not to retrace their steps in order to face the Egyptians. The Egyptians, in fact, had already been faced and defeated. To spend energy on reliving that fight would have detracted from fulfilling their destiny.

In many cases, fighting is required. But Moses tells the Israelites not to fight: "Stand firm." Moses realized that the desire to get involved in a war with the Egyptians was irrational and driven by fear. Fear will often drive a person to move in the wrong direction. Moses was telling the Israelites not to allow fear to dictate which direction they went. He was asking them to stand firm against the urge to move in a direction that would hurt them in the long term. Going to war, in this instance, would be going backwards at a time when moving forward was vital. To these warriors, Moses was in effect saying, "This is a time to face your fear, trust and move forward—not a time to use your fighting skills, which will ultimately drag you in the wrong direction."

THE RECORDING INDUSTRY: FIGHTING A WAR WITH ITS OWN CUSTOMERS

Sometime in 2006, marketing executives invited a group of teenagers to their headquarters in London. The teens, wearing the latest low-slung jeans and cocked baseball hats, were asked to sit in a conference room and listen to clips of different music and then give their opinions. At the end of the focus group session, the executives thanked the teens and brought in a big box of CDs to pay them for their time. The executives told the teens to take as many CDs as they wanted—for free. The teens looked at the discs, but all of them left the room empty-handed. "That's when we knew the game was up," one of the executives told a reporter for *The Economist* magazine, who wrote about the meeting.

Ever since the MP3 revolution began hitting teenagers' earbuds in the late 1990s, the music industry has been in trouble. By creating a purely digital version of a song—a version which could be transferred freely across the Internet in a matter of seconds—the MP3 heralded the end of the music industry as we know it.

The only problem was that the industry executives didn't hear the trumpet blast. Instead of adapting to the new situation and rebuilding their business around digital sales, they attacked their own customers through advertising campaigns and lawsuits.

The impact of digital music started to affect industry sales in 2001, as online services sprang up to serve as brokers between people who wanted to trade digital music files. At first these services, with names like Kazaa and Limewire, hardly had an impact on CD sales. By 2002, however, the industry experienced its first annual decline in CD sales, dropping from $13 billion in 2001 to $11 billion in 2002. The record companies huddled together and decided that it was time to respond. So they authorized their trade group, The Recording Industry Association of America (RIAA), to start tracking down online music traders and sue them.

The strategy had legal merit: anyone who uploaded a music file that was digitally copyrighted was officially breaking the terms of the contract that went into effect when they bought the CD. But the RIAA soon discovered that they were attacking their most treasured asset: the relationship with their customers. Teenagers were hauled into court and charged with a crime that they didn't even realize they were committing. Single mothers, grandparents, and school administrators—those who owned the computers on which someone else had downloaded a music file—were ordered to pay fines in the tens of thousands of dollars. The perception of the music industry in the minds of music lovers changed from that of providers of entertainment to that of litigation-crazy moneygrubbers. Civil rights groups and self-organized boycott groups sprang up to defend those being sued and denounced the music industry in the press.

But the music corporations had a bigger problem with their strategy: it wasn't working. Digital downloads kept growing, while CD sales continued to plummet. They continued their legal attack, but they also conceded to online sales—allowing the computer company Apple to start selling songs digitally on the internet for 99 cents a pop on its iTunes service with the caveat that the digital files be encoded with digital rights management (DRM) software, which restricted users from playing the song on any device they chose. Music buyers responded enthusiastically and iTunes became a big hit, but its sales still couldn't replace all the lost CD sales. Too many digital music users didn't want to be hampered by the DRM software.

It wasn't until late 2007 that the music industry finally threw in the towel. By the end of that year, each of the five largest companies had agreed to start selling DRM-free music online. In the first two months of 2008, their turnaround appeared justified because downloading music is increasingly becoming the way music connoisseurs buy their music. This is evidenced by the fact that CD sales continue to fall while the downloading of legal music continues to rise by an average 50 percent each year.

So now music customers and music corporations are on the same page. The industry will still probably get lower revenues because there will always be people willing to download pirated files for free rather than pay a reasonable price for them. But at least there will still be a music industry. If they had waited much longer, the entire business might have simply disappeared. That's what happened to the CD-store business—today there are less than one-fifth the number of CD stores in the United States than in 2000.

So no harm done, right? Wrong. The music companies had chosen to sue their very best customers, instead of offering DRM-free downloads for sale at the very first sign of trouble. This created a wall of distrust between themselves and their customer base that may never go away. Instead of moving forward in the face of change, they chose to set their sights backwards and fight. That fight took a lot of their resources (all those lawyer fees they had to pay) and focus. More importantly, it caused them to lose the trust and allegiance of their customers. Few people have sympathy for an industry that was suing grandmothers and thirteen-year-olds.

Much like the group of Israelites who called for a battle on the banks of the Sea of Reeds, the music industry turned around and looked for a fight instead of moving forward and looking for other more creative options. They sued several thousand individuals and spent millions in legal fees. But they didn't win the war. In the end they were forced to do the one thing which they had resisted so strongly—sell digital downloads that were not restricted by DRM. But in the process, they wasted resources and goodwill that could have been used to form a new social contract with the music-buying public at the dawn of the MP3 age.

INSIGHT FOR BUSINESS: *Fighting battles takes energy that is often better spent being productive. Remember that fighting is a backwards motion. Concentrate on going forward instead.*

INSIGHT FOR LIFE: *Fear can cause you to want to fight when doing so can have the opposite of the desired result. When facing an adversary, whether your teenager or spouse at home or your boss at work, pick your fights very carefully. Whatever the case, stand firm against fear-driven reactions that urge you to fight.*

Retreat

Let's return again to the Israelites at the sea. Given the circumstances, the faction that advocated a return to bondage must have appeared the most reasonable. They knew they could remain alive in Egypt, however miserable such a life was. They knew that, if nothing else, life could go on. Even though they had come farther than any of them could have imagined, the concept of backtracking must have sounded pretty appealing.

Moses clearly understood this and did not try to shame them. He did not try to artfully appeal to their noble, fearless side—there wasn't time to sway them that way. He also did not try to convince them that it was all an illusion—that if they clicked their heels three times and closed their eyes the enemy would disappear.

Instead, he acknowledged the situation as it was and painted a brighter picture of hope to give them reason to choose a different path. "Though you see the Egyptians now, you will never see them again," he said. In effect he was saying that our eyes aren't fooling us. Those really are Egyptians bearing down on us. But the desire to return to Egypt as slaves is not a justified response. "You are making them larger than they really are and the fear is therefore exaggerated," Moses was saying to them. He was reminding them that God was on their side and had just defeated mighty Pharaoh for them. Moses was trying to put the threat into perspective for the Israelites, telling them that with God on their side the defeat of the Egyptian army would be instantaneous. Moses tells us that fear drives our minds to overstate the threat.

So often our fear causes us to want to return to what is familiar rather than to face challenges. That's because the threat of the unknown appears much larger than it really is. Moses yet again imparts timeless wisdom—that fear enlarges all potential threats beyond their true proportion. Once you realize this, you can move forward with confidence that the future has much better potential and the past will fade into obscurity. In other words, when the going gets tough, realize that fear makes threats look larger than they really are and there is no need to retreat to what is familiar. Remember the strength you had to leave the past and move forward with faith.

Note that the thought of returning to Egypt would have taken the Israelites' attention away from the task at hand: journeying forth.

A word of caution: the faith to continue on despite the odds cannot be blind. One must make an educated decision as to which direction is forward. The Israelites knew that walking into the sea was forward because their leader, Moses, had told them so. Unfortunately, you do not have a Moses to tell you what to do. As you move forward, make sure your decision to do so is based on a proper understanding of what is involved, and that the decision is backed up with real information and knowledge. Moving forward based on blind faith may in fact result in moving backward.

GENERAL MOTORS: PLAYING BY YESTERDAY'S RULES

When General Motors announced its 2006 lineup of new models, attendants at the Detroit Automobile Show weren't very surprised. If anything, the SUVs were heavier, the pickup trucks were bigger, and the economy cars were even less visible. GM had ridden the SUV craze to record sales figures for the last five years and it wasn't about to stop.

Someone forgot to remind GM's executives that gas prices had skyrocketed in the last year and did not show any signs of returning to their previous levels. A year later, for the first time in the history of the auto industry, Toyota pulled even with GM in terms of the number of cars sold. The always mighty GM was no longer the largest carmaker in the world.

Toyota had succeeded by concentrating on the problems of today. Their models offered significantly better gas mileage than GM's. Instead of focusing on the SUV as its primary model, Toyota put its branding resources behind the Prius—the revolutionary electric/gas hybrid car that can get sixty miles to the gallon.

While many analysts today criticize GM for its shortsightedness, the real motivation behind the company's faulty strategy was fear. GM executives were happier staying in a place that was familiar, too afraid to try something new or to question the assumptions on which their SUV strategy was based. Instead of moving forward, they inspected the previous year's sales figures and decided they were comfortable with that. This strategy caused them to wrongly assume that the next year's sales would follow the same path. It did not, and the company suffered as a result.

It seems that Toyota was taking Moses's advice—it was not looking over its shoulder at GM, nor was it reverting to what was comfortable and familiar. It did its homework and then had the confidence to be innovative. Toyota had the conviction to move forward.

Very often, fear causes inaction at a time when action is vital. Lack of action is the culprit in just as many corporate mistakes as taking the wrong action. Remember that experience is vital, but familiarity is not always the right guide when it comes to business or life.

INSIGHT FOR BUSINESS: *Fear makes the unknown seem more ominous than it really is. Sticking with strategies of the past can often hurt a business. The world is always changing—manage for today and tomorrow instead of yesterday.*

INSIGHT FOR LIFE: *Always face the future, not the past. You need no longer fear the enemies that you have already conquered.*

Learned Helplessness

The final group arguing before Moses, those who pleaded to pray for God's deliverance, had very good reason to believe that such a strategy would work. After all, these were the people who had seen countless miracles in Egypt. No other group of people had ever before or after witnessed so many irrefutable acts of God. Prayer to that God would seem like a good choice in this situation.

But Moses admonished this group, too. "You shall remain silent," he told them.

It's not often that a prophet tells people not to pray. But there was a good reason for Moses's command. An important act had to be done. The Israelites were required to walk forward into the water. God would not move their legs towards the shore. Moses could not lift each one of them and throw them in. The onus was on each and every Israelite, man, woman, and child, to act.

Praying, on the other hand, is an act of personal introspection and communication with the divine. When you pray, you avoid any other activity and concentrate wholly on the prayer. Prayer in a time of trouble is also an act that demonstrates complete reliance on something other than your own actions, in this case God.

People pray for a whole host of reasons. Some pray to bless God. Others pray to thank Him. And some pray to request something of Him. But God never expects us to pray without action. If something needs to be done, you can pray for it, but only if you intend to actually do something about it as well. Here Moses was saying that prayer motivated by fear with no intention of acting is futile. As long as you are alive, you can act and make a difference. There is never a situation that calls for praying and then waiting for a miracle. There is always something that can be done. Praying that the action will succeed is perfectly suitable, but prayer with no intention of doing something to help the situation is unacceptable.

Fear can cause us to feel unable to act on our own. Instead we demand that others act on our behalf. It is not surprising that the Israelites wanted to abdicate their responsibility to take action. Only a few days before, they had been slaves. Every decision had been made by someone else. Physical punishment and verbal abuse had been constantly thrown at them. That was how it had been their entire lives, from birth to that moment on the shoreline.

The urge to rely on others is also known by psychologists as "learned helplessness." People who have had no control over their lives and have suffered abuse have a tendency to react to a crisis by curling up into a ball and giving up. It's not just ex-slaves that tend to do this, either. We all suffer small injustices at work, social settings, and elsewhere in our lives. We learn to shut down our hearts as a way to endure the suffering.

This cycle of behavior turns life into an endless string of painful events. Shutting down one's heart might seem easier than living through the pain, but it's just another form of surrendering to fear. Here Moses tells us to be silent and resist the urge to depend on others to take over. Face the fear and act. Once you take responsibility and move forward, others can help.

Moses is warning us here not to allow our fear to cause us to leave our lives solely in the hands of fate, or even God. The wisdom is profound. The first step out of a fearful situation must always be taken by us. After that, help will come. But we must take one step forward and then things will happen in ways that are never anticipated.

CRAMER, BERKOWITZ, & CO.: A REFUSAL TO SURRENDER

Jim Cramer was having a bad day on October 8, 1998. The hedge fund that he co-managed with his partner Jeff Berkowitz was being squeezed by a stock market that was spiraling downward and a host of angry investors who wanted their money back.

Cramer, who has since become a television celebrity from his CNBC market commentary show *Mad Money*, was at the time an extremely successful hedge fund manager. Over the course of fifteen years, his fund averaged 24 percent annual growth. He did this by trading in and out of volatile stocks multiple times every day, taking advantage of quickly rising or falling prices. He would buy and sell if he thought a stock was about to go up, or he would short-sell (bet against the stock) if he thought it was about to go down. His encyclopedic knowledge of the markets allowed him to make a fortune on a daily basis. By early 1998 he had grown the funds under his management to more than half a billion dollars.

But in 1998 he appeared to have lost his touch. That summer, a succession of bad calls had pushed his portfolio into negative territory for the first time in his trading career. Then the international debt crisis exploded in September when the failure of another hedge fund, Long-Term Capital Management, pushed the entire bond market to the brink of disaster, causing his holdings to plummet into double-digit-loss territory. By October, his fund was down 38 percent for the year.

In normal times, Cramer would have had another two months to fix things—according to the bylaws of his hedge fund, he did not have to report his performance until the end of the year. In addition, his investors had to wait until the end of the year to withdraw their money.

But 1998 wasn't an ordinary year for him. In order to appease an investor who needed to withdraw his money, the fund had opened its vault for a special one-time withdrawal on October 8th. Any investor who wanted to his or her money back on that day could do so. When Cramer had agreed to the special redemption day, the market was performing well and his investors showed no sign of mistrust. But at the height of the debt crisis, rumors were circling Wall Street that his fund was about to go bankrupt.

So on the morning of the eighth, Cramer had a major problem. A large group of investors were demanding their money back that evening—in the form of cash—while all the stocks that he owned were dropping like boulders. He had one day of trading left to try to restore his portfolio to a higher value and then give his investors back their cash.

Due to the crisis, Karen Cramer, Jim's wife, had returned to her spot on the trading desk that day. Cramer, who refers to his wife as the Trading Goddess, had learned the business from her back in the late 1980s, when she was his chief trader. They had worked together for more than a decade, until she retired to raise their daughters. Karen had been away from the trading desk for six years when she returned on that morning to help her husband attempt to avoid bankruptcy.

The morning began with the market moving in the same direction that it had been moving for weeks: downwards. Investors were terrified that a real economic depression was looming. They were selling their stocks at any price they could get. As the morning wore on, Jim realized that his time had run out—he had to start selling his stocks in the midst of this panic. He had to meet the evening's deadline with whatever money he could get.

Karen overruled him. She had been watching the stock ticker and was astounded that the stock prices of so many excellent companies with exceptional profits were so incredibly cheap. Instead of selling, she commanded the firm's traders to buy. Her husband could not take it anymore. He counteracted her command and ordered his traders to put in a 5,000-share sell order on most of the stocks they owned. And then repeat that order every sixty seconds. Keep doing it, he told them, until everything is sold.

After twelve years of running his fund masterfully, Jim Cramer had given up. The golden boy of Wall Street had finally been beaten by the markets he had found so easy to defeat in the past. He walked back into his office, closed the door, and began to write a commentary for the Website www.thestreet.com, in which he opined that it was time to give up and sell everything. The big one had finally come. October 8, 1998, he wrote, was as bad as the 1929 stock market crash. He remembers thinking about the stock brokers who leapt to their deaths from New York City skyscrapers that day sixty-nine years earlier. For the first time in his life, he would write later, he understood why they had done it.

Then something on the television screen caught his eye. Ron Insana, the CNBC announcer, was announcing that the Federal Reserve might lower interest rates in order to salvage the stock markets. For the first time, the Dow reversed course and was up 20 points in a matter of seconds. Cramer emerged from his office and returned to the trading floor. His traders were fielding buy orders from everywhere. The Dow kept climbing.

Cramer and his wife quickly agreed to cancel the sell orders and start buying. Now that their portfolio was rising, they could easily borrow the money they needed to pay off their investors who were pulling out of the fund. The eighth of October, it turned out, was the absolute bottom of the stock market's fall. Karen Cramer had been right. Jim Cramer had been wrong. Dead wrong.

Years later, he would write about the events of that day in his memoir, *Confessions of a Street Addict* (Simon & Schuster, 2002). He wrote about how he had asked his wife why she had been so confident that the market was about to rebound that day. How, he asked her, was she so sure that the market had reached a bottom? Her reply, as Cramer recounts it in his book, was:

"Because at the bottom, even the coolest, most hard-bitten pros blink. At the bottom the last bulls throw in the towel. At the bottom, there is final capitulation." She waited until it dawned on me who she was talking about. "At the bottom, Jimmy, you capitulated. At the bottom you gave up . . ."

Over the course of the next two months, Cramer, Berkowitz & Co. continued to ride the upturn in the market. By year's end, their fund was able to report a 2 percent increase in the value of the portfolio for the calendar year. Cramer proudly points out that those investors who stayed in the fund that October saw a 200 percent increase in their holdings over the course of the next two years.

The one day in his professional life that he surrendered, Jim Cramer was fortunate enough to have put his wife in charge of the trading desk. For a few minutes he had overridden her orders and given up. He had given up all hope and abandoned himself to fate. But he ultimately learned from Karen, after many years of being told he was the smartest man on Wall Street, that there's never a good time to surrender. Karen Cramer had internalized the same idea Moses had conveyed to the ancient Israelites when they were seemingly at rock bottom with the Egyptian army chasing them from behind and the sea closing the path in front of them—don't give up or rely on fate, just move forward.

Jim Cramer retired from the business a little more than two years later to spend more time with his wife and daughters. Later, he would start a second career as a highly successful broadcast journalist. But he still recalls October 8, 1998, as the day he learned the most important lesson in his life: Never, ever surrender your business to the whims of fate.

INSIGHT FOR BUSINESS: *A good businessperson never surrenders his or her business to fate. The moment that you start blaming* *unseen forces (the market, currency traders, Chinese imports . . .) is the moment that you relinquish control.*

INSIGHT FOR LIFE: *Never forget that you are responsible to act. Others can give you guidance, but neither they nor God should act for you when you're capable of doing it yourself. No matter how strong your belief in God or others, they won't help you if you are not trying to help yourself.*

Journey Forth!

After Moses spoke, the Israelites were stuck with a dilemma. The command he gave was very simple: "Journey forth!" Executing that command also was simple: just start walking into the water. But their fear told them this wasn't a good idea. Their instincts told them they would surely drown. Emotion told them to give in to their fear.

It was then that the Israelites did a miraculous thing: they conquered their fear. By realizing that the source of their desire for defeat was fear and that their fear was blowing the threat out of proportion, and by not giving in to the urge to fight and not being paralyzed by resignation, they chose to move forward. They chose to go into uncharted territory rather than back to what was familiar. With a well-founded faith in God and in Moses, both of whom had proved to be trustworthy in the past, they walked straight into the water.

As frightening as those first steps must have been, they overcame the paralysis that had come upon them, raised their feet, and placed them into the water. We all know what happened next—a miracle occurred and the sea split. Some people dismiss the story of the parting of the Sea of Reeds as impossible. Others claim there is some obscure scientific reason why the waters receded that day. But such debate isn't very productive, because it misses the point of the story. The Israelites conquered their fear and stepped into the water even though their pulses were racing, their muscles told them to stop, and their fear tried to pull them back. That's when other opportunities opened up for them. And thanks to the description of paralyzing fear and the correct responses to it found hidden within this small biblical passage of the Torah and its corollary commentaries, it's a feat that can be repeated anytime, anywhere, by anyone.

INSIGHT FOR BUSINESS: *Eliminate fear from all decision-making. Use risk-analysis to quantify danger instead of reacting to generalized fears. Miracles occur only after you face your fear and move forward.*

INSIGHT FOR LIFE: *Recognize that perception changes once you dip your foot into the water. Insurmountable odds don't look so threatening once you have moved forward and embarked on your journey.*

Meditation

This chapter has focused on fighting against the fear of making major changes and journeying toward the unknown. First, determine in which way you and your business ought to move forward and which fear reactions are standing in the way of that progress. Then consider which of the four categories of fear—self-sabotage, fight, retreat, or learned helplessness—your circumstances fit. Once you have identified your reaction to your fear, ask

yourself how Moses would respond. Once you have the answer, you can be-
gin contemplating. Reframe in your own words the response you have con-
cluded Moses would give into a short couple of sentences that suit your
circumstances and begin to contemplate them using the meditation guide at
the end of the book.

The Real Answer
Cut your Loses And
Buy the winna's

CHAPTER 2

NOTHING STANDS
BEFORE THE WILL

Harnessing Willpower to Succeed in Business

Nothing stands in the way of a person's will.

—THE MYSTICS

MOTIVATION ISN'T JUST AN ASSET THAT IS USEFUL IN ACHIEVING success—it's a prerequisite. Without motivation, failure is guaranteed. But how do people motivate themselves towards success? Most advice reverts to old clichés like "Knuckle down and bear it," "Put your nose to the grindstone," and "Hard work conquers all." While these nuggets of wisdom do contain kernels of truth, we can all cite examples in our own lives where they simply did not work. If you have built your own business you know that to succeed, you need to be a self-starter. For that, pure determination and endurance is not enough. Something else is required to reach your goal—and that is passion.

According to the Torah, that missing piece isn't that hard to find: it's already inside you. The Kabbalists wrote about something they called *"pnimiyut ha-ratzon,"* which can be translated as "inner will" or the "authentic self." It's not out in the open, but wrapped up in something called the *"chitzoniyut ha-ratzon,"* or the "outer will," which often veils the authentic self.

Once you've found your inner will, *then* you can put your nose to the grindstone, knuckle down, and follow every other euphemism you've ever heard for working hard. Passion, motivation, and success will follow.

Just find your authentic self. It's that simple. Okay, maybe it's not that simple. Finding your authentic self involves a lot of hard work, too. But it's within your grasp, it's within everyone's grasp.

This may come as surprising news for most people in our society. We're taught to get a career and stick with it. Sadly, this often leads to midlife crises as we reach middle age only to find our lives are empty. No sports cars, no speedboats, no mansions are going to fill the void if our authentic self is not aligned with our career choices.

The philosophy of the Torah offers a path for the person in search of his or her authentic self. Once you find your authentic self, it becomes an endless spring of motivation and passion for whatever you want to achieve in business and in your personal lives. To find the inner will and passion that will lead to your success, you must start at the very beginning.

Two Divine Desires: An Inner Will and an Outer Will

The Torah begins with the words (Genesis 1), "In the beginning God created heaven and earth." And we cannot help asking, "Why did He do it?" In trying to answer that question, the Torah sages analyzed God's actions and words and the narrative tale of how He created the world. In the process of that analysis, the concept of inner will and outer will, of *pnimiyut ha-ratzon* and *chitzoniyut ha-ratzon,* was developed.

Despite the detailed narrative that describes the creation of the universe in the Torah, the text doesn't explain why God created the world. It does not say "God created the world because He wanted power," or that "God created the world because He was lonely." Yet humans yearn for an answer. If we are God's craftwork, why did He choose to make us?

According to the mystical teachings of the Torah there are two parts to God's desire to create a universe: an inner will and an outer will. An outer will can be more clearly explained as an action that, for one reason or another, we are required to take. It's an element of will because when performing our outer will, the inner will is reflected. Think about moving your office, for example. If your inner will is to have a bigger and more spacious workspace, included in your outer will are the necessary acts of finding a space, signing a lease, creating a layout, and schlepping your furniture.

So God's outer will in creating the universe involved forming light, darkness, water, dry land, vegetation, seed-yielding herbs, fruit trees, the sun, the moon, and living creatures.

But remember that according to the mystical teachings of the Torah, the creation of the universe was only an expression of the Divine *outer* will. The universe was created not for its own sake but for a higher, inner, purpose. The universe for its own sake has no utility to God. He created it to achieve a higher overarching aim. To reach that higher purpose, a universe in all its diversity was needed.

In common with any creative process, God needed to use His outer will and create a universe that could achieve the higher aim He had in mind. Thus, nothing was left to chance. No detail was left out. Every aspect of the universe was fully thought out and masterfully designed. It had to be this way if it was to fulfill its inner purpose. And when everything was finally completed and in place, God was ready to introduce the main aspect of creation, the most sophisticated item He was to create: the human being. But even the human being was part of God's outer will. Yes, even we humans were created solely in order for God to achieve His ultimate aim.

There are many opinions about God's ultimate reason for creating the universe. The most accepted explanation comes from a midrash that says God desired a dwelling place on a plane that was seemingly devoid of divinity and He wanted humankind to recognize Him. In other words, God wanted recognition and therefore created a universe. Whatever God's reason, according to most Torah sages, the particulars of the universe were created by God's outer will and as such do not have an independent reason for existence but are here to serve a higher and inner Divine desire and will.

Thus, as it was for God, the outer will is the element of our desire that does not seem directly related to the ultimate goal that we really want to achieve—our inner will. However, expressions of the outer will lead directly to the accomplishment of that inner will.

Elon Musk: Becoming the Rocket Man

In the fall of 2006, Elon Musk sat in a room near a beach on an island in middle of the Pacific Ocean, watching an image of a space rocket on his laptop's screen. A few hundred yards away, the actual rocket stood, wisps of vapor rising from its metal skin in the tropical sun. Inside the rocket were thousands of pounds of frozen oxygen sitting next to compartments of kerosene.

This is what he had wanted to do ever since he was a boy in South Africa. As the countdown proceeded, his mind focused on the image. The rocket was his baby; he had paid for it with his money and he had managed the elaborate process of designing it and building it. But now it was time for launching it. One of his employees was actually going to push the button. It was Musk's turn to watch.

Watching has never been one of Elon Musk's strong points. When he first became intrigued by computers, he quickly found out that he had more fun programming the code for video games than playing them. As he neared adulthood, his parents sent him abroad, afraid that he might be drafted into the apartheid-era South African army. Musk went to Canada, and later to the United States, to pursue an education in computer engineering.

After completing two undergraduate degrees at the University of Pennsylvania, Musk chose Stanford for his post-graduate work. He lasted two days. It was the golden age of the Internet, and he had ideas for how to create new industries through it.

It took Musk four years to build his first company, Zip2, into an organization that the computer company Compaq bought for $370 million in 1999. He was considerably faster with his second company, PayPal, which he sold to eBay in 2002 for $1.5 billion.

While Musk had always been fascinated with computers and making them more efficient, he knew that his destiny was tied to space. After the PayPal sale, he decided to solve the single greatest problem of space travel: getting out of the atmosphere cheaply.

Since the 1960s, NASA hasn't been able to lift a pound of material to outer space for less than $10,000. Musk thought he had figured out a rocket design that would undercut that price by a factor of five. Ever since his schoolboy days, he had dreamed of being part of the space race. Now that he was worth several hundred million dollars, he had the means to compete.

After several years of development, the company that Musk founded, called SpaceEx, was ready to finally test launch the rocket he had invented, the Falcon. An earlier attempt had resulted in the rocket exploding shortly after launch. But he identified the flaw that caused the explosion and the new Falcon was ready to go. Visitors from several government agencies and corporations had flown to the Kwajelein Atoll, the site of the SpaceEx launch pad, to see whether this crazy Internet guru could put metal into space.

"Five . . . Four . . . Three . . ." Musk watched his computer screen. The rocket looked just like the ones he had daydreamed about as a boy in South Africa. "Two . . . Liftoff!"

Amidst fire and smoke, the rocket rose up into the clear blue sky and then quickly went out of sight. According to signals from the sensors on board, the rocket went well beyond Low Earth Orbit, the spot that was the goal for this test.

The launch was a success. Musk and his team had proven that they could lift material into space at a price point that had never before been achieved. After spending countless millions of his own dollars, his company now had a clear path to becoming the FedEx of space delivery. The day, it turned out, wasn't too bad for the man and his rocket.

For Musk, his Internet businesses had been part of his outer will. They were only a means to the end of realizing his inner will that had now blasted into space and was blazing towards a bright future.

A good starting point on your own journey to find your inner will is to look at your own workday.

In the course of an average workday, what activities lead directly to you inner goal and which are merely necessary tasks that have no connection to that inner goal? This is not to suggest that the tasks related to your outer will are a waste of time; some of them are necessary if your inner will is ever to be actualized. Life simply doesn't work if you fail to attend to the difficult tasks that need doing as well.

Think of this as a mental exercise. Let's say that in the average day you fill out your travel expense report, reply to colleagues' e-mails, make two or three cold calls to find new clients, do online research into a topic that you need to know about, sit in a meeting with your team, etc. . . . Which of those tasks lead directly to inner goals?

What if you can't find any relationship between your inner will and tasks you do at your job? Most likely that's a sign that it's time to start thinking about a new career that will be more in keeping with your inner will.

INSIGHT FOR BUSINESS: *Don't wait for luck to bring you the job of your dreams. You will find it through self-awareness, long-term strategic planning, hard work, and sacrifice. If you know what you want, then prepare to sacrifice and work hard to reach that goal. In the end, you will.*

INSIGHT FOR LIFE: *Spend time each day thinking about whether your life is in sync with whatever your inner will wants to achieve. If it is not, start planning a way to make the two roads to merge.*

Two Desires in Creating a Business:
An Inner Will and an Outer Will

Building a business is somewhat like creating the universe: it involves both an inner and an outer will. You cannot go wrong if you follow God's example, for God is the ultimate entrepreneur and His enterprise is the universe.

Like God, all people are entrepreneurs. For those of you who haven't started your own company, restaurant, store, etc., your career should be viewed as your entrepreneurial enterprise. However much it might seem that your fate is controlled by others, it is you who hold dominion over that part of your life.

All too often we enter a profession because of its convenience. We say we took the job because it was available at the time. We fall into all sorts of careers because of what was offered rather than because it was what we really wanted to do. In our work lives, few of us actually work and do business in fields about which we are most passionate. This leads to mediocrity and a lack of fulfillment.

The inner and the outer will can be illustrated by the example of driving to work. The actual driving is the outer will but arriving at work is the inner will. The outer will is necessary to achieve the inner will.

When you start a new business you need to do the market research, write a detailed business plan, raise capital, hire qualified staff, rent office space, buy equipment, and attract clients. All of this is a lot of detail work and not always much fun. But, you can't succeed without following the outer will, which then allows the inner will to be achieved. No business can survive without a proper infrastructure. But the infrastructure is only a means by which the business can thrive. It's through the outer will that the inner will can be achieved.

Unfortunately, all too often the outer will takes over and becomes the main focus of attention. In order to succeed, we must keep our eyes firmly on the inner will and on our passion.

Teachers often go into teaching because they love helping students progress and they have a passion for educating in a classroom setting. Often, as teachers move up in their careers, they become less involved in teaching and more involved in management. This is just one example of how the outer will can overtake the inner will. The management and administration of a school is pure outer will; it is only there to allow the inner will, the educating of students, to exist. When a good teacher becomes an administrator, the inner will is offered up as a sacrifice on the altar of the outer will. The reality is that being an effective administrator requires a different set of skills than those used by an excellent teacher. It's a waste of good teaching talent to use an effective teacher for administrative purposes. In order for schools to run properly, talented teachers should remain in the classroom and good managers should steer the administrative aspect of the school.

Business is no different. To be profitable, a business must maintain its focus on its primary goal—profitability. To be successful in business, you must never allow the surrounding aspects of your business life—the meetings, the memos, the forms, the phone calls, the e-mails—to distract from the passion that motivates you to work hard in the first place. Doing this will result in a loss of motivation.

One of the most important aspects of success is focus. There are so many things in life that can distract us from goals; that can cause us to forget what we first started out to do. The outer will has a knack of doing that to all of us. Driving around town without a destination is unfulfilling. Similarly, getting sidetracked by the outer will causes a loss of motivation and fulfillment which in turn will hurt your business's bottom line.

Howard Hughes Medical Investigators Become Managers

The Howard Hughes Medical Investigators foundation (HHMI) is an enormous fellowship program that chooses the best medical scientists in the world and then pays their salaries so that they can concentrate on doing scientific research (as opposed to writing grants, looking for jobs, attending faculty meetings, and the like). HHMI wanted to find out how their scientists were spending their time. So in 2002 they polled their hundreds of fellows throughout the world.

The poll indicated that the average HHMI fellow spent less than 10 percent of his or her time in the laboratory doing research. Despite the liberation given them by their HHMI grant, they still spent the vast majority of their time in meetings or managing the workers in their laboratories. Instead of freeing up precious time, an HHMI fellowship more often than not led to an increase in the size of the lab and the number of technicians and junior scientists being employed, and therefore the management tasks expanded. These brilliant scientists had ceased doing research and instead spent their time managing people. Their outer will had taken over.

> INSIGHT FOR BUSINESS: *Having a high position that demands respect doesn't mean that you are realizing your inner will. Never forget what makes you passionate, and work towards spending time doing it. Active reflection about yourself will help you keep in touch with your inner will. Magically, it also helps you perform the tasks of the outer will that are necessary in order to achieve the goals of the inner will.*

> INSIGHT FOR LIFE: *Recognize the differences between your inner will and your outer will. If you are staying true to your inner will (such as having a happy and fulfilling marriage), the acts of the outer will (such as remembering to take out the garbage), become so much easier to perform.*

Discovering Your Inner Will

To enjoy your business life or career and remain motivated to continue with it, the inner will must always be the focus of your attention. But for many of us, the question is what the inner and authentic will really is. How can we know what we are really passionate about? According to the Kabbalists, it is a soul thing: we are passionate about things that are closest to our authentic self. Unfortunately, many people have disguised their authentic self to such a degree that they no longer recognize that it exists. So the first and most important thing to do is to get in touch with it. This is easier said than done, but it is vital if real and sustained success is ever to be achieved.

The first thing to do is to become aware that the authentic self really does exist. Once you have acknowledged this, you are halfway there to finding it. The second thing to do is to realize that the authentic self does not always follow logic. This does not mean that you cannot find a logical reason for what the authentic inner desire expresses. You usually can. However, the basis of the expression of your authentic and inner will and desire is not intellect or logic—it is pure soul-speak.

The expression of the authentic self can be exemplified by the love a parent has for a child. This love is not dependent on anything else. In most cases it will always be there. Even when the child may act in a way that is hurtful to the parent, the parent still feels love for the child, because that child is their flesh and blood, and the love is not based on any benefit they derive from the relationship with the child. The parent-child relationship is a quintessential bond that transcends any intellectual reason. In a similar vein, an expression of our authentic self cannot necessarily be logically explained. Very often we feel that we want something but the reason for it is not immediately apparent. This may be because we have just experienced and expressed our authentic self.

Clearly, though, the soul does not want just physical pleasures and fulfillment. It craves spiritual fulfillment. As we will explain in Chapter 7, according to the Torah, spirituality is very much compatible with the creation of personal wealth. When we look deep within, we find that at the core of our basic needs for fulfillment are two central issues: first, helping others, and second, a connection to something other than ourselves.

These two desires lie at the center of everyone's innermost will. How they manifest will vary from person to person. For one it might be through helping the poor or through prayer. For another it might be through building a company that makes vital contributions to the lives of people. For yet a third, through the intellectual pursuit of deeper or higher knowledge. Each person will find that his or her inner will embraces these two basic needs and desires—

helping people and striving to connect to something other than the self. If your passion has nothing to do with either of these two aspects, it's most likely not coming from your inner will and will not lead to complete fulfillment.

Another way to identify your authentic self is to recognize when you become completely engrossed in something. If you are able to jump into a subject or action to the degree that you lose all sense of time and feel a deep sense of fulfillment, you know that that subject or action aligns with your authentic self.

Whenever the authentic self express itself, the senses are heightened and the ability to focus and achieve is greater. The authentic will and desire of true musicians is to play music. They therefore excel at it, and are able to play endlessly without getting bored. Their motivation is high because they are doing something that expresses who they are on the deepest level. Each of us has something in our life at which we can excel. Each of us has something that expresses our authentic self. The secret is to take that thing which you are most passionate about, the thing which most clearly is an expression of your authentic self, and make a business out of it. The details of how to carry this out will differ depending on what your inner will is, but the general parameters are always the same: think about the commercial application of your inner will and authentic desire, and then market that.

The final thing to know about an expression of the authentic self is that it always wants to be creative. One of the fundamental drives of the human being is to create a new reality—one that did not previously exist. It's true that businesspeople want to make money, but behind the desire to become financially successful is the craving to be creative, to create a set of circumstances that did not exist before. In this sense the goal is yet again to emulate God's creativity on the road to success and fulfillment.

INSIGHT FOR BUSINESS: *Realize that your inner will should be your primary focus in everything you do in your business life. This isn't just a spiritual exercise, to be done in an occasional weekend retreat or in a therapist's office. Modern life may have fooled us into thinking that uncovering the inner will is a luxury—but it's not. It's a desperate necessity. Without it, success in business will remain a step away.*

INSIGHT FOR LIFE: *Find your authentic self and then follow it. This is the only way to find true fulfillment.*

Combining Passion and Pleasure to Succeed in Business

Some might assume that because the particulars of the universe were only a part of His outer will, God may have become impatient with the menial process of creation. In fact, the opposite was true. Numerous times throughout the creation process we hear God saying (Genesis 1:25 and 31) that "it is good" or "it is very good." This is taken to mean that God felt immense satisfaction in the creative process even though it was only a means to achieving his main goal and not the goal itself.

In Genesis (1:27), it says that God created humans in His image. Torah commentaries understand this to mean that each and every one of us is, in a sense, a mini-God. They say that humans share God's attributes but in an infinitely smaller way. So if we follow how God acts, we will reach similar conclusions. In this case, if we follow our authentic inner will then we, too, will gain fulfillment and true satisfaction from carrying out our outer will. A good example of this is resting on the Sabbath. According to the Torah, God created the world in six days and on the seventh day, Saturday, He rested. God then asked that people rest on the Sabbath as He Himself had rested. This is because He wanted us to emulate Him. And if we emulate God, we will be able to reach the ultimate success and fulfillment that we crave (more about emulating God as a means to succeed in business in Chapter 9). Similarly, if we follow God's example and identify our authentic desire and passion and then follow it, we will still enjoy doing the other things along the way that are only directly related to that passion and desire.

Also, as we previously mentioned, when you follow an inner will and desire you lose all sense of time and self, which means that you are having a really good time. This is what the ancient Torah sages meant when they said that pleasure is always present when we are carrying out something that is in step with our inner will. The pleasure, however, is so subtle that we don't really feel it. Unlike eating a good steak or spending a day in the spa the pleasure is not overt; there is no immediate gratification of the senses. Nonetheless the pleasure is there. It is a covert pleasure, yet ever so powerful.

The benefits are clear: if we really enjoy what we are doing—whether in business or in our personal life—we do it with increased enthusiasm and vigor. This is the other benefit of following our inner will and desire: the work itself becomes enjoyable. Going into the office becomes fun rather than a burden. The rule is that whenever the authentic inner will and desire come into play, subliminal and subtle pleasure also are present. When we feel motivated and fulfilled by our work, and at the same time derive pleasure from it, success is never far away.

Follow Your Authentic Will and Overcome Procrastination

Every business and career includes aspects that are enjoyable and aspects that are more monotonous and boring. Doing tax returns or inventory assessments is a necessary and time-consuming part of most businesses. But if it is all part of serving the inner will, then the monotonous tasks take on a different meaning—they become much more important and less boring.

For an enterprise based on inner will to be successful, administrative tasks are vital. Simply put, just doing what one is passionate about all day will not make a successful business. There's a lot of other work involved to make a business profitable. The problem is that the work one is less passionate about—the outer work—becomes less of a priority and therefore gets neglected. The only way to combat this is by keeping an eye on the ball. You must never forget that if you want to achieve your dreams, and if you are, in fact, following your inner will and passions, then the outer aspects of your career and business are important. If you keep this in mind and make it part of your thinking, then the more monotonous aspects of your business will take on a whole new meaning. When your outer will becomes attached to your inner will—when they both become two sides of the same coin—then the outer aspects of your business life will become infused with the same motivation, and will provide the same fulfillment, that the inner will does.

When this happens, you can look around at the work of your outer will and be satisfied with it. After finishing a long tax return or inventory assessment you can say "it is very good." You can feel fulfilled and satisfied with your work even though it is not the work you are most passionate about. This attitude and feeling of contentment will directly affect your business's profitability, because when you find something fulfilling it often also becomes more enjoyable, helping you to complete your tasks quickly and on time. A common example of this is people who say that they have a passion for travel. Do they really enjoy spending hours and hours on a plane, car, or bus? It's unlikely. They are passionate about visiting new places and encountering different cultures. They say they love traveling because traveling is the outer will that leads them to the inner will of visiting new places. Because it is seen as an integral part of the inner will, the traveling itself—which is pure outer will—becomes fun and infused with passion.

One of the biggest challenges many of us face is procrastination. We procrastinate on chores that are important because they are not enjoyable. Most of us try to do what is most enjoyable first and what is least enjoyable last. In this way, the least enjoyable chores keep getting postponed, even when there is time to do them. Procrastinators always find other more "enjoyable" things to do instead. When important but not enjoyable aspects of our business are pushed to the back burner, it eventually affects the bottom line. If, however, you can find even the menial aspects of their business enjoyable and fulfilling, then you will act more efficiently, and productivity will rise as a result. This is what King Solomon meant when he said (Proverbs 22:29), "Have you seen a man quick in his work? He will stand before kings; he will not stand before poor men."

One of the keys to real wealth and business success is to work fast and not procrastinate. One of the secrets to overcoming procrastination is to find delight in everything you do. In business, the way to do this is to see the direct connection between the outer will and the inner will and take notice how the outer will guides you directly to the inner and passionate will.

INSIGHT FOR BUSINESS: *The best antidote to procrastination is to enjoy doing your work. By ensuring that your outer will is in sync with your inner will, the menial tasks will become more meaningful—and easier.*

INSIGHT FOR LIFE: *Don't seek the overt pleasures in life and overlook the things that give you deeper and more subtle pleasure. By*

*following your inner will and desires you can live a life filled with
a constant stream of subtle pleasure and enjoyment.*

Andy Klein's Crisis of Will

In the beginning, Andy Klein fulfilled the image of the perfect son
of a Jewish mother: A bachelor's degree from Brandeis. An Ivy
League law diploma. A job as a securities lawyer at Cravath, Swaine
and Moore, one of the toniest of Wall Street law firms.

For several years, Klein filed endless memos, letters, and papers regarding his clients' initial public offerings (IPOs). If you had seen
him on the subway heading to his apartment after another long day
at work, you probably would have thought he was just another Wall
Street "MOU" (that's "Master of the Universe," for those who have
never had the good fortune of meeting a Manhattan investment
banker who uses that label to describe himself)—rich, lucky, and
pompous.

Then, in 1992, on one of his weekend getaways to Europe, Klein
ordered a traditional wheat beer from a country inn and took the
glass outside, where he lay down in the grass to enjoy the view of the
rolling Belgian hills. Just as he took a sip of the beer, a revelation fell
from the sky and landed directly on his head. Andy Klein, it said, is
not a happy man. He took another sip of the beer and somewhere
in the midst of his admitting that fundamental truth to himself,
Klein had another thought: This is the best beer I have ever tasted in
my life.

Back in Manhattan, Klein could not shake the two thoughts out
of his head. Despite his impressive income, he had lost his passion
for work. And he could not get that beer out of his mind, either. So
he did what any sane person would do: he quit his six-figure job and
began to brew beer.

The passion was back, and soon too was the fine taste of that Belgian wheat-based beer. After learning the secrets of the Belgian brewmeisters, Klein figured out how to do it himself. He opened a small brewery—this was in the days before the term "microbrewery" had been coined. And then he started a company around it, called Spring Street Brewery.

Within a short period of time he was serving his expensive but incredibly good beer to bars throughout lower Manhattan, where most of the customers were lawyers and investment bankers who were prepared to pay a premium price to drink Klein's beer. His business continued to grow.

Still, something was gnawing at him. He had lost his passion for practicing corporate law, but it seemed a shame to waste his legal skills and talents. The beer company was doing fine on its own and was getting to be so successful that a public offering of shares was necessary to raise funds to reach the next level.

But when the investment banks turned up their noses at underwriting his IPO, Klein knew he had to get creative. He knew the business of IPOs and knew he could raise more money if he could reach investors directly.

So Klein executed the first Internet IPO in 1996. Without using an investment bank, he offered shares in Spring Street Brewery at a fixed price to investors through the brewery's Website. Within days, he had raised $4 million. And he did not have to pay a penny to an investment bank.

Klein's direct IPO raised so much interest in financial circles that he soon formed a new company, called Wit Capital (named after Spring Street's flagship brew), to advise other firms on Internet IPOs. Soon the company morphed into an investment bank, and, in 1999, his new bank had its own IPO, which raised $80 million.

Since retiring from his bank a few years after its IPO, Klein has moved to Amsterdam, where he spends his time mentoring new start-ups. His latest is an online advertising company, Spotzer, which provides customizable video clips for local advertising on the Web.

It's easy to summarize Klein's story as being about someone who left a soulless Wall Street job to find contentment in beer. But that's the wrong way to look at it. True, Klein made money in beer, but he also returned to investment banking. The fact is that investment banking isn't inherently soulless, and it's a vital part of our economy. Investment bankers make key decisions on how to allocate capital. When they make the right decisions, the overall economy runs more efficiently, more jobs are created, more health care bills are paid, more sons and daughters get sent to college, etc.

But it's easy to lose sight of that when you are doing it for the wrong reasons. And in Klein's case, he was doing it in the first few years of his career simply because it was what was expected of him. When he left the investment banking industry, he realized there was a way to do it better and more cheaply than the traditional banks. And he made another fortune off of that.

It would be audacious for us to suggest that Andy Klein received spiritual enlightenment through drinking a glass of beer, and that's not our message either. Something inside Klein was telling him that he was out of touch with his inner will. By listening and acting on that inner voice, Klein was doing something whose secret is found in the Torah's creation story. He was making sure that his outer will was in congruence with his inner will and authentic self. And then he began to have fun as well.

INSIGHT FOR BUSINESS: *Find your inner will and the expression of your authentic self and then use that talent as the focal point of your business endeavors.*

INSIGHT FOR LIFE: *Make a note of the things that you feel most passionate about. Make a note of the things that cause you to lose track of time when doing them. Figure out which of them are expressions of your authentic self and then plan how to emphasize those things in your daily life.*

Nothing Stands in the Way of Your Authentic Will

Many books offer strategies for handling the menial aspects of business. Some proclaim that you need to be organized, get the difficult and boring things done first, and then give yourself the reward of doing the enjoyable things afterwards. This strategy takes a tremendous amount of energy and discipline, forcing you to slog through tasks that are monotonous and boring. The strategy we outlined above is much easier. When you have a combination of passion or and pleasure in even the menial and boring parts of your work, success inevitably follows. Clearly, the easy way to succeed is by actually finding joy in everything you do. When this happens, work ceases to be a chore and becomes a pleasure. And few people lose motivation or burn out from having too much fun.

Harnessing the power of the will can help everyone overcome major challenges. Have you ever heard someone say that they willed something to happen and it did? Well, the secret is that the inner will has an incredible amount of power. There is an age-old saying that comes from the Torah's greatest mystical text, the Zohar, which states that "nothing stands in the way of a person's will." Clearly there is much wisdom inherent in this statement and it parallels the English saying of "where there is a will there is a way." The depth of this statement is regrettably lost on many people, and the same people have no idea how to harness willpower to achieve their goals.

This is because those people did not understand what the great mystics meant by the word "will." They did not mean that if you wish strongly enough for a new car or a bigger house you will eventually get it. They meant that if you act in accordance with your inner will you will achieve your deepest desires. The statement attests to the power of the inner will and the effect it can have on your motivation and passion to achieve what you really want in life. You must realize that what you *really* want is not necessarily based on any social or cultural influence but on what your soul dictates. Getting in touch with your soul and realizing what it wants for you is the most powerful thing you can achieve on the path to success. You must look within, not without.

When you identify what the inner will wants, and recognize how it can manifest, there is nothing that can stop the will from becoming a reality. The reason for this is now clear: the inner will causes you to become passionate and motivated to fulfill its desire so that even the menial aspect of it becomes pleasurable. Nothing can come between the power of the inner will and success. The great thing about real success is that financial rewards almost always accompany it. Indeed, nothing stands in the way of the inner will.

> **INSIGHT FOR BUSINESS:** *The inner will is one of the most powerful sources of energy that exists in this world. Discover your own and the path to success becomes clearer and shorter.*

> **INSIGHT FOR LIFE:** *Your innermost desires have to do with two things: helping others and getting in touch with something that is higher than yourself.*

Meditation

This chapter laid out the path towards getting in touch with your inner will and passionate desires. Spend time contemplating the things you have expe-

rienced in your life that have been ultimately fulfilling. Find the things that you have really enjoyed doing. Think how you can fit them into your business life or how you can turn them into a business. Contemplate the menial and monotonous aspects of your career or business and find how they lead directly to the fulfillment of your inner will and passionate desire. As you contemplate these things, feel the motivation for fulfilling your inner will swell up inside yourself. Savor that motivation and get on with the job. Most of all, make sure that you have fun doing it.

CHAPTER 3

THE HUMBLE PATH
Taking Ego Out of the Entrepreneur

He who is willing to humble himself, the hour of success awaits him.

—MIDRASH

EGOTISM IS ONE OF THE GREAT UN-TALKED-ABOUT FEATURES OF the business world. What motivates a person to start a new business, create a new product line, or enter into a new career? Money, of course, plays a part. But the promise of riches usually isn't enough to outweigh the risks that are taken on starting something new. Egotism plays an important role, too. It's a driving force behind every human endeavor, from romances to wars to IPOs.

Yet it's hardly ever discussed. We seem only to talk about ego when we're complaining about someone's overabundance of it behind his or her back. Torah-inspired writings, however, contain explanations, debates, essays, and even action plans for how to address ego and its ugly stepbrother, egotism. The rabbis accepted healthy self-esteem as a necessary human attribute. They also aligned different forms of ego along a spectrum—just like other human capacities and emotions. They understood that there are different manifestations of ego, ranging from narcissism to humility.

The Torah disagrees with the conventional wisdom in our broader society, recognizing that some forms of pride are actually beneficial to an individual and to society. This conflicts strongly with modern cultural norms, which implore us to act and speak in an artificially humble manner while rewarding us for letting our egos rage behind closed doors.

The Torah counsels us to fight against the urge to place ourselves above others or above God. And it defines a type of humility that rises—counterintuitively, to our modern ears—out of self-esteem.

The business world can learn a lot from this way of thinking. Its ways are very different. Egotism is too often rewarded. Too many battles are fought in boardrooms and in office hallways, where the result is that the victor gets an ego boost and the vanquished loses dignity. The health of the business suffers because people who should be leading it higher are instead wasting their time fighting over turf.

Successful business owners always have one thing in common: they find the proper mix of humility and healthy self esteem. That ideal recipe isn't printed in any self-help books or available on eBay. But it's discussed openly in ancient Jewish texts. Let's explore what the texts of past millennia said about ego and humility, and where it fits into success in business.

But first a note about a word in this chapter's subtitle: entrepreneur. As with this entire book, the wisdom and insights aren't limited to entrepreneurs. But having an entrepreneurial mindset is helpful if success in anything is going to be achieved. Whether you have opened your own donut shop or you work in a government agency or a multinational corporation, your quickest route to success is to consider yourself an entrepreneur. The market into which you are trying to sell and advance yourself might be different, but only the scrappy, self-driven person with hunger and dreams (i.e., one with the entrepreneurial spirit), is able to taste success.

So let's delve into the Torah concepts of pride and humility, and how to balance them to make your ego work for you. We'll start with the starkest example of arrogance that the Torah has to offer.

Pharaoh the *Gas Ruach*

The Egyptian Pharaoh who enslaved the Biblical Israelites is an excellent example of a *gas ruach*, a Hebrew word that means a person of coarse spirit. A more meaningful translation would be an arrogant person whose self-love is based on inflated or nonexistent foundations. The Pharaoh saw himself as a god with godlike powers—an infinitely inflated sense of who he really was. His adversary Moses, conversely, had the opposite trait—humility. In fact, the Torah says (Numbers 12:3) that Moses was the most humble person on the face of the earth.

But in what way was Moses humble? The first story the Torah tells about Moses (Exodus 2:11-12) as a young man is how he killed an Egyptian because he did not like the way the Egyptian was treating an Israelite. The very next day, the Torah relates, Moses saw two Jews fighting and said (Exodus 2:13-14), "Wicked one, why are you hitting your fellow?" To which they respond, "Who placed you as a judge and minister over us? Are you going to kill us as you killed the Egyptian yesterday?" From day one it seems that Moses was perceived by others to be arrogant. So why does the Torah say Moses was so humble?

The teachers of the mystical aspects of the Torah answer that Moses had the following attitude that made him so incredibly humble. Moses assumed that if anyone else had been given his attributes and his talents they would have achieved results far better than he could have. There is tremendous wisdom here. Moses was aware of who he was and the talents that he had. He had what we might call healthy self-esteem. He also knew that he had a very lofty position and was destined to become a great leader. Moses was realistic about his role and even demanded that others show him respect. However, this did not make him an arrogant *gas ruach*—he did not have an inflated opinion of himself nor did he have illusions about his own importance. Moses did not take any of the credit for what he had achieved. He realized that all his abilities and gifts were God-given. He knew his mission and wanted to carry it out to the best of his ability.

A practical difference between Moses's humility and Pharaoh's haughtiness is seen in their respective reactions to God's requests of them. When Moses met God at the burning bush and was asked to go to Pharaoh to demand the emancipation of the Israelites, he responded by asking (Exodus 3:11): "Who am I?" Moses was expressing his own sense of humility and was questioning his own worthiness as God's personal messenger to Pharaoh. In the end, Moses realized that God wanted to send him especially, and therefore acquiesced.

Conversely, when Moses told Pharaoh that God wanted the Israelites freed from slavery, Pharaoh asked incredulously (Exodus 5:2): "Who is the God that I should listen to his voice?" Notice that while Moses was questioning his own worthiness, Pharaoh was questioning God's worth and importance. Torah sages compare this to the verses in Isaiah (47:8–9), which says: "Now hear this, you who are used to pleasures, who sit securely, who says in your heart: 'I am, and there is nothing beside me; I shall not sit as a widow, neither shall I know the loss of children'—but these two things shall come to you in a moment in one day, the loss of children and widowhood; in their full measure they will come upon you."

These verses describe the depravity of the *gas ruach*, who thinks that they are completely in control of everything to the extent that they say "I am, and there is nothing beside me." They don't believe in God and they think that all the good they have is the fruit of their own work. This is what the Torah warns against when it says that one should not say in one's heart (Deuteronomy 8:17), "My strength and the power of my hand has made for me all of these possessions," thereby forgetting that everything is a blessing from above. The *gas ruach* highly overestimates their own power and abilities and thinks that they are, in effect, standing in the place of God.

Ultimately the abovementioned verse in Isaiah warns that this type of self-centeredness only ends in destruction and tears. This was the case with Pharaoh, whose inability to realize that there were forces infinitely bigger than himself brought about his own and his country's demise. The same is true in all areas of life and business: people who have a highly inflated sense of their abilities and talents and are delusional about their place in the world will eventually fail.

In both business and life it is vital to be realistic about our abilities and talents. It's frustrating to hire people to do a job they say they are competent to do, only to find out that they overestimated their abilities and didn't do the job right. People who do this will not get repeat business and their bottom line will suffer. People who are dishonest about what they can do will always end up being poor businesspeople who lack the trust and respect of others.

Moses's response to Pharaoh is instructive as a prototype method of handling a *gas ruach*. Moses did not allow Pharaoh to intimidate him. He was firm and made the consequences of Pharaoh's delusions clear, saying that if he did not become pragmatic and listen to God, he and Egypt would suffer. People who are unrealistic about their own abilities, talents, and position in the world must be firmly

brought back to reality and made aware of the ruinous consequences of their delusions.

Countrywide Financial: The Credit Crunch and a
Gas Ruach Mortgage Company

It's not all that hard to choose examples of the *gas ruach* tempera-
ment in modern business. Just take a look at the headlines. In the
midst of the worst housing slump and ensuing credit crunch, examples of unfounded arrogance abound. From the misplaced calm of
the Bear Stearns managers right before that firm collapsed to the repeated denials of trouble by the municipal bond insurance companies prior to their plummets in valuation, the winter of 2008 has
certainly proven that the spirit of the *gas ruach* is alive and well on
Wall Street.

One firm, however, stands head and shoulders above the rest in
the scope and the brazenness of its arrogance. Countrywide Financial, the world's biggest mortgage originator, was, for five years, one
of the best stocks to own, appreciating at an average rate of 35 percent a year from 2001 to 2006. It's no coincidence that those years
coincided with the U.S. housing boom. That was the secret to Countrywide's success: as home prices increased and as the volume of
mortgage origination exploded, Countrywide could do no wrong.

Angelo Mozillo, the co-founder and CEO of the company, rode
the wave of the housing boom like an expert surfer. Although he
rarely bought shares of the company, he was its single largest share-
holder because of shares that had been awarded to him as part of his
compensation. By mid-2007, according to a *New York Times* article,
he had sold large chunks of those stocks for a total profit of $406
million.

None of that, of course, is wrong in and of itself. A good manager
like Mozillo who oversees such a long period of expansion and prof-

its should be rewarded handsomely. However, it was in the management style that he exhibited after the housing market began to dive that the *gas ruach* inside of Mozillo really began to show—and its destructiveness knew few boundaries.

For one thing, just as housing prices started to head south in late 2006, Mozillo and his management team decided to double up the intensity of the firm's efforts to sell subprime mortgages. These high interest loans for people with low credit scores were only a tangential business for Countrywide in the past, accounting for only a few percentage points of its revenue. But subprime mortgages were too lucrative for Countrywide management to pass up, so, according to a *New York Times* story that appeared in August 2007, they ordered their sales force to steer customers in that direction.

But in their *gas ruach*-induced arrogance, Mozillo and Countrywide seemed oblivious to the massive additional risk from the subprime mortgages. Mozillo insisted that Countrywide managers knew what they were doing. According to a story in The *Wall Street Journal*, unbelievably, he said a few years before the bubble burst that his firm would continue to rise in any market: "I'm fairly confident that we're not going to do anything stupid. We have a history of not doing anything stupid."

The higher proportion of subprime mortgages in their portfolio made Countrywide a greater credit risk. And by the end of 2007, that came back to haunt them. As home prices plummeted and the credit markets froze, Countrywide suddenly couldn't borrow money to lend out as mortgages. And its preexisting mortgages dropped in value dramatically. Countrywide's stock fell alongside the value of its portfolio, losing more than half its value in 2007.

And what was Angelo Mozillo doing in the meanwhile? Issuing pearls of wisdom to the financial press, crowing about how his team of experts would profit from the crisis. Even as the bubble was bursting, he continued backslapping his management team. "This will be great for Countrywide," he told CNBC in March of 2007, "because at the end of the day, all of the irrational competitors will be gone." It apparently didn't occur to Mozillo that his own firm's intense push into the subprime market was itself an irrational action.

By 2008, Mozillo's glib talk had evaporated, as had his company. When Bank of America finally agreed to buy Countrywide in January, the price of the deal was about $4 billion. That's less than 10 percent of Countrywide's valuation at the end of 2006. While Mozillo seemed to have done well with the sale, getting more than $100 million in severance pay, he still might have to face judgment on his stock sales and his corporate leadership: both the FBI and the SEC are investigating Mozillo and Countrywide for possible criminal behavior in regards to predatory lending practices and securities law.

While Angelo Mozillo is surely no Pharaoh (his sins are pretty minor compared to mass enslavement and attempted genocide), his *gas ruach* tendencies hurt himself and his company. He clearly showed that he knew how to manage the company when times were good. But he was unable to recognize his own limitations and lack of experience in managing a large company during a real estate downturn. This illusion of grandeur led to the evaporation of most of Countrywide's valuation in a little less than eighteen months. If he had known his own limitations, Mozillo might have brought in a better management team and sought advice from those who understood the real estate market better. Instead, like any *gas ruach*, he arrogantly believed in and even boasted about his business invincibility, and Countrywide shareholders were left to suffer.

INSIGHT FOR BUSINESS: *No one likes to be around a* gas ruach. *Finding a mentor, a financial backer, a partner, or even a supplier will be hard for such a person. If you detect that behavior in yourself, fight it. Nothing will kill your hopes of success more* *quickly than being a gas ruach. Likewise, when you detect it in others, gently try to put them in their place and explain the potential consequences of their arrogance. If this does not work, avoid them. In the long run, they will not have much to offer you.*

INSIGHT FOR LIFE: *Unfounded pride—being a* gas ruach—*is bad for your soul too. By refusing to acknowledge God's presence in your life and crediting everything to your own wonderful self, you distance yourself from the opportunity to taste spiritual fulfillment.*

Korah the *Ba'al Ga'ava*

Another type of arrogant person described in Judaic texts is the *ba'al ga'ava. Ba'alai ga'ava* (the plural—and there sure are plenty of them) are realistic about their abilities, talents, and achievements and, unlike the *gas ruach*, probably have good reason to be proud of themselves. However, they have an immensely inflated sense of self-importance. In fact, *ba'alai ga'ava* are so self-centered they are unable to see the needs of others—all they see is themselves.

The classic Torah example of a *ba'al ga'ava* is Moses's cousin Korah (Numbers 16). During the time the Israelites were camping in the desert some three-and-a-half thousand years ago, Korah incited a mutiny to challenge Moses's leadership. At the behest of God, Moses had granted the position of high priest to his brother, Aaron. It was a position that Korah had expected to be given. Two hundred and fifty distinguished members of the community joined Korah in his rebellion, complaining that Moses was taking the best positions for himself and his brother Aaron.

Now the Torah concedes that Korah was a holy man who had a highly developed sense of spirituality. He was, in his own right, a truly great person. By realistically assessing his own talents and achievements he knew that he was suitable for the job of high priest. Based on this he went ahead and challenged Moses for the job he coveted but which had been given to Aaron.

To our modern-day sensibilities it seems that there was nothing wrong with Korah's behavior. In most western counties this is the way political leaders are selected. But the Israelites in the desert weren't a liberal democracy. They had agreed to live by the word of God, and it was God—not Moses—who had chosen Aaron to be high priest. Korah had no right to challenge God's choice of high priest. His motivation for rebelling against Moses was not pure. The sages maintain that Korah's mutiny was the prototype of an argument that was (Ethics of the Fathers 5:17) "not for the sake of heaven." In other words, the dispute had a selfish motivation. Korah wanted a top job and was willing to do whatever it took to get it, even if that meant disturbing the peace and causing distress to the community.

This is what a ba'al ga'ava does. While realistic about their own talents and achievements, they are willing to do whatever it takes to get what they want for themselves, even if it means that others will suffer. Ba'alai ga'ava are so self-absorbed that they do not recognize that their actions hurt everyone.

In Moses's response, his humility directly contrasts with Korah's arrogant behavior. Instead of putting down the revolt by killing or imprisoning Korah and his men, as some leaders may have done, Moses began a dialogue with him to resolve the issue. He was not offended by Korah's revolt. To Moses, nothing was ever personal. All he cared about was the will of God and the interests of the people he was serving. Moses offered to stage a competition, the winner of which would get the coveted job.

Ba'alai ga'ava, on the other hand, will sabotage their own and others' success to achieve selfish aims. In business, they are not to be trusted to do the right thing. They are unable to make a decision that only benefits the business if it does not benefit them as well. *Ba'alai ga'ava* do not know how to be team players, and as a result their businesses suffer.

We can learn from Moses how to handle these people as well. Do not simply dismiss them. Due to their past successes, they often have real influence, abilities, and talent, and they can cause significant damage to relationships and organizations. Take their complaints seriously and do not allow them to become the basis of an ego battle. Allow for proper dialogue, but make sure that you have the ability to prove beyond doubt to the *ba'al ga'ava* and his or her followers the error of their ways so that if you need to discipline them in some way you have the weight of evidence and fairness behind you.

Korah's end is illustrative, too. As he and his supporters gathered to confront Moses, God split open the earth and buried them alive. While Moses was willing to discuss things he was also firm when Korah did not relent to a reasonable argument and serious consequences followed. Although the earth rarely swallows people up anymore, a metaphorically similar fate often awaits the unrestrained *ba'al ga'ava* today as well.

Long-Term Capital Management: Reading Your Own Press Clippings

John Meriwether is an example of a *ba'al ga'ava*. Given an enormously powerful position of authority based on his real talents and admirable successes, he lost sight of his own fallibility.

Meriwether started out as one of Wall Street's heroes. He was a bond trader at Salomon Brothers during the 1980s and early 1990s. He pioneered dazzlingly complex trading strategies that made his firm, his clients, and himself spectacularly rich. In a field that prizes intelligence, Meriwether was considered to be the smartest of the smart.

So when he left Salomon in 1994 to found his own hedge fund, it wasn't difficult for him to attract a billion dollars in starter capital. He soon drew more investors by hiring renowned mathematicians, some of them Nobel Prize winners. By the beginning of 1998, Meriwether's firm, Long-Term Capital Management (LTCM), had more than $5 billion in investments.

In reality, Meriwether was in control of a lot more money than that. He and his team had identified a method of arbitrage between domestic and international bonds that could make a little bit of money at very low risk. But Meriwether did not want just a little bit of money. To maximize his ability to generate income, he leveraged his portfolio, borrowing money from other Wall Street firms to invest along with the money he already had under his control. He then became involved in complex derivative trades that exposed his company to even higher liabilities.

In order to continue his tradition of compounding his clients' money by 40 percent annually, Meriwether borrowed as much as 100 times the amount of his investors' money from other Wall Street firms. The banks' willingness to lend him such an enormous amount of money was a tremendous trust, and his abuse of that trust created negative reverberations all around the financial world.

The investing models designed by Meriwether and his Nobel prize-winning employees seemed to guarantee that he would make a killing. He could cash the investments in, pay off the loans, and still boast of stratospheric returns for his clients.

The Russian government, however, had other ideas. In the spring of 1998 it responded to its own economic troubles by simply walking away from its debt. As a result, other emerging countries' debt markets plummeted. Meriwether was caught with a lot of worthless bonds while his negative bets against U.S. treasuries were losing value, thanks to everyone fleeing to their relative safety and therefore bidding up their prices.

As Meriwether pleaded with his investors for more money to pay off his loans, the rest of Wall Street realized that something was wrong at LTCM. As the scope of the disaster began to become clear, the entire global financial system started to shudder.

It would seem that the world's markets—cumulatively worth close to $30 trillion in 1998—would have been big enough to withstand the bad decisions of a single trader who was running *only* $5 billion. But that's not the case when that trader had bought derivatives with borrowed money. And not when the liabilities for those derivatives reached a stunning $1.25 trillion. Had the global financial markets collapsed, John Meriwether of Greenwich, Connecticut, would have owed more than a trillion dollars—a debt he could not possibly have paid back.

As the stock markets of the world dropped and the bond markets seized up, the federal government paid a visit to Meriwether's office. It was clear that his clients' investments were now worthless and that, if forced to sell his portfolio at a time when all the potential buyers had disappeared, he could cause an even worse panic throughout all the globe's stock markets. Alan Greenspan, the chairman of the Federal Reserve, came to him with an offer. Greenspan had cobbled together a group of billionaires and investment banks who were willing to buy the holdings of Meriwether's firm from him at their depressed prices and then would hold onto those positions until they returned to their proper valuations. It was a way of keeping the financial world from suffering the consequences of one man's folly.

Meriwether hesitated at first, but then capitulated and agreed to the rescue. His investors got back pennies for every dollar they had originally invested in LTCM. And he earned a place in history as the man whose blindness to his own fallibility almost broke the back of the world's financial system.

Perhaps the most telling moment of the affair was when one of Meriwether's deputies, who was trying to describe how a firm filled with so many smart people could have made such bad investments, claimed that it wasn't the firm's fault. According to their models, he said, the only way for the investment to fail was if a "ten Sigma" event occurred. That's math-speak for multiplying a billion by a billion, moving the number "1" from the left side of the resulting number all the way to the right side, and then putting a decimal point in front of the very first zero. Another way of looking at it is that if an event had a ten-Sigma probability of occurring every second, it would probably happen only once in the course of six billion years.

As Nassim Taleb, a New York University professor of finance and a frequent critic of LTCM's even before its crash told a *DerivativesStrategy* magazine reporter about LTCM's hubris: "Ten Sigma is supposed to occur so infrequently the probability of your model being wrong is far greater." The inability to see that, Taleb said, wasn't a miscalculation. It was "blindness."

From Taleb's analysis of LTCM, it seems that Meriwether and the people that helped him manage LTCM were undone by their overestimated sense of self-importance, which blinded them to their own limitations. Like Korah and his group of mutineers, Meriwether and the LTCM people were capable and talented. But they were too willing to risk the health and safety of others (their investors, the investment banks from whom they borrowed, and, for that matter, the entire global financial system) for their own misguided goals. In other words, they had no qualms about taking everyone else down with them—a classic *ba'al ga'ava* trait.

INSIGHT FOR BUSINESS: *You might have a very good reason to be proud of yourself. But just because you are so great does not give you the right to do harm to your business or your team. Never lose sight of the reasons you have been given a position of authority—stay true to them.*

INSIGHT FOR LIFE: *Do not allow your talents or abilities to get the better of you. Always remember that they are gifts from Above that are meant to be used fairly—never use them to control others. Always serve the interests of the greater goal, not your own self-interests.*

Moses: The Most Successful Entrepreneur of All Time

Now let us return to Moses to gain more insight into the definition of humility. Moses saw the sufferings of the Israelites in Egypt and took action. On God's order he challenged the Pharaoh and won. At God's behest he led the Israelites out of Egypt in a most miraculous way, which included the raining down of the famous ten plagues upon the Egyptians until they relented. Moses understood his mission and carried it out with single-minded determination. His enterprise was to take a nation out of slavery and transform it into one that would eventually make massive contributions to humanity. He was one of the world's most successful revolutionaries and his vision was, at the time, unique.

According to the Torah teachings, Moses was the greatest intellect ever to live (Guide of the Perplexed 1:54), and one who had regular discussions with God (Numbers 12:6–8 and numerous other places). There have been very few people in history more successful than Moses. Even in publishing, Moses was spectacularly successful. The book he ghost-inscribed on behalf of God—the Torah—has been a bestseller for well over three thousand years.

As mentioned earlier in this chapter, Judaic sources do not attribute Moses's stunning rise to his intellect or to his oratorical abilities (in fact, Moses had impaired speech). He may have been an amazing strategist and tactician, but even these are not seen as his most praiseworthy attributes. According to the Jewish tradition, his greatest asset was humility.

The following story from the Torah illustrates this humility and is very instructive to the business person. Moses's father-in-law, Jethro, was a powerful tribal leader as well as a chieftain, a scholar, and a mystic. When Moses became Jethro's son-in-law, he was a fugitive on the run from Pharaoh's wrath and had not yet had a revelation from God. Jethro was an idolater and Moses was a believer in monotheism. Needless to add, these were factors that could not have been conducive to a wholesome father-in-law/son-in-law relationship.

Often when in-laws disagree, each side can become entrenched in their own views, unwilling to see the other's perspective. Moses and his father-in-law did not see eye to eye on most things. Yet it seems that they did not get ensnared in this trap. As soon as Jethro heard about the miraculous splitting of the Sea of Reeds and the wonders that God performed for the Israelites upon leaving Egypt, he realized that his son-in-law's theology was correct and his own religious beliefs were flawed. He immediately traveled into the desert to learn from Moses and to find the truth. When he arrived, a warm and respectful encounter ensued (Exodus 18:7): "Moses went out to meet his father-in-law, and he bowed to him and kissed him, and they asked each other about their welfare and they came into the tent."

After hearing—first hand—about all the miracles that God had performed for the children of Israel, Jethro did not resent the fact that he had been mistaken and his son-in-law's theology had been proved right. On the contrary, "Jethro rejoiced because of all the goodness which the Lord had done to Israel." He made a dramatic turnaround—denouncing idol worship with the words (Exodus 18:11), "Now I know that the Lord is greater than all gods."

The very next day (Exodus 18:13-26), in true father-in-law style, Jethro criticized Moses's leadership and gave him unsolicited advice. Jethro saw that Moses stood all day judging the people, and there was a long line waiting for him; some had to wait from morning until evening to get an audience. Jethro told Moses that he should delegate the judging process to others. Many family feuds have started because an in-law offered unsolicited advice or criticism. Moses, however, was unperturbed. In fact, he was grateful for the sensible advice and implemented it immediately.

The ability for these two strong personalities to have such a wonderful relationship and show each other such respect and admiration lies in their humility. This does not mean that they did not realize their greatness; they did. But they knew that there were things beyond themselves—a greater truth that needed to be grasped and understood. Moses and Jethro were both humble. They did not allow their egos to get in the way of doing what was right. Jethro felt that he had found truth with idolatry, but being a quintessential truth seeker, once he saw the errors of his ways he was more than willing to change.

Moses was no different. When Jethro pointed out to him that as the solitary judge of his people he was not serving them efficiently, he was grateful for the advice and then made the necessary improvements. Neither cared from where or from whom the truth came; the fact that it was the truth was all that mattered.

But Moses's ability to follow his father-in-law's advice, and to give him the credit for it by naming an entire Torah portion after him, is more remarkable than Jethro's acknowledgment that Moses was right about theology. Moses had proven his ideas. God had split the sea for him. With the help of God he had defeated the mighty pharaoh and was now leading his people through the desert for a rendezvous with God at Sinai. Jethro had no such track record, and Moses could have just ignored his advice and would have been justified in doing so. But that was not who Moses was. He was humble, and when good advice was given he was more than willing to accept it no matter from whom it came. The lesson is clear: humility has nothing to do with the way one stands or holds oneself. Humility is the ability to see beyond the self. Humble people can do things that don't directly benefit themselves and may even detract from themselves for the sake of the bigger picture and others.

Often people will interpret healthy self-esteem and pride as arrogance. We *should* know our qualities and be proud of them. It is just as important for us to be fully aware of our talents as we must be of our shortcomings. Real arrogance has to do with an inflated sense of our own abilities or importance. As we shall see, understanding this definition of arrogance is a vital part of being successful in business.

So ego can be both a positive and negative character trait; how, then, are we supposed to tell the difference between people who are healthily proud of themselves and those who are arrogant? The Torah sages had an answer for this question. They proposed a simple test: see how the person reacts to being insulted.

The practical difference between the arrogant person and the healthily proud person is that a person with an inflated sense of self-importance will become easily offended and will harbor a grudge. Arrogant people—whether a *gas ruach* or a *ba'al ga'ava*—have sensitive egos. Although they are happy to belittle others and show how they are better, when others do the same to them, they get very offended and hurt and then remain bitter and hold deep-seated grudges—the arrogant person's ego never heals.

Humble people, by contrast, upon being insulted may initially be very hurt, but within a short period of time will get over it. They will think deeply about the insult and what it means to their personal life, and how they may use the new-found information gleaned from the insult to become a better person. As they realize that the insult may have some utility, they stop being angry towards the person who insulted them. For humble people it is not about themselves and their ego. It is all about what needs to be done for a higher cause. For egotists, it is all about them and their importance and abilities; nothing else counts in their eyes.

Like Moses, the truly humble person has a clear picture of his or her own abilities and talents and is able to accept the criticism and advice of others without getting offended. This was the key to Moses' success as a leader. His own sense of self-importance did not impinge upon the mission at hand. Moses was able to easily work together with others for the greater good. For him there was no such thing as an ego battle. If something needed to be done and it was correct to do, Moses would do it. Ego never got in the way of doing what was right.

In business, this humble attitude is vital for true success. Successful enterprises are a work of collaboration between stakeholders and customers and employees. The arrogant businessperson who is unable to take criticism will not benefit from this sort of collaboration. People will not feel comfortable sharing their concerns and ideas with an arrogant boss, because nobody wants to offend the person who is responsible for their livelihood. Too many businesspeople see their enterprise as a testament to their abilities and talents and as fulfillment for their egos. If they changed focus and saw the business as a means to making their vision come true, rather than a means of boosting their ego, they would be more successful.

Cisco Systems: Overcoming Ego Clashes in Silicon Valley

In 1984 Len Bosack and Sandy Lerner, computer administrators at Stanford University, knew that they had a good idea for a company.

The network they were helping to administer was becoming enormous and needed to communicate with other networks on the campus. But each network had its own protocol (set of instructions for use—almost like a language). They devised a machine which could take messages from any network and send them along to any other network, even if the network's protocols were different.

So the two left academia and invited a large group of talented engineers and programmers to join their company—later to be called Cisco Systems. All the people involved in the start-up were brilliant in their own fields. But they weren't necessarily chosen for their ability to get along with others.

Those early days of Cisco Systems were often described in history books as the time that the Internet matured. The Cisco machine was dubbed the multiprotocol router. It allowed multiple networks to join together and, just as the founders had envisioned, a revolution was born.

But that's not to say that working in such an exciting environment was much fun. In those early years, personalities clashed and egos warred. One early employee said that the five founding members would go for months at a time without speaking to each other due to petty disagreements and turf wars.

It wasn't until John Morgridge, a former Air Force officer and computer industry veteran, was brought on as a CEO in 1988 that the company was able to overcome its internal tensions. When Morgridge took over, Cisco Systems had about thirty employees and only $5 million in sales. Two years later, the company had more than $1 billion in sales and over 2000 employees.

What was Morgridge's secret to managing a motley cast of egos into a winning team? A belief in the need to put ego aside for the greater good. Because of this, he always mediated disputes with compassion and justice. Like Moses, Morgridge did not care about his own ego being bruised. He cared about doing what was needed to fulfill the goal. In Cisco's case, the goal was growing the company. Morgridge compelled team members to concentrate on the skill sets at which they excelled. He forced everyone to work for the good of the company, not towards their own selfish ends.

Morgridge could have taken over the leadership position at Cisco Systems and then engage in the same egotistical behavior. Instead, like Moses, he chose to take his authority and use it to focus the team's talents and attributes towards growing the company. And grow it did. Today, Cisco Systems has a stock market valuation of more than $180 billion, making it one of the ten largest companies in the world. And Morgridge is still the chairman emeritus of the company.

There is, however, an important concept to keep in mind when talking about humility. There is a big difference between being humble and being a doormat. The latter is only harmful to any enterprise. We should not allow others to tread on us. We are all obligated to stand up for our rights.

Let us return to the story of Moses and Korah to get some deeper insight on this. Despite his humility, Moses would not just roll over and allow this megalomaniac named Korah to ruin the society that had been carefully built. Instead, Moses dealt with him in a firm but fair manner.

If we take the Moses model as an example, one finds that, although he was humble, Moses did not allow others to undermine the mission he was trying to achieve. When the Israelites were wandering in the dessert and Korah and his men rebelled against Moses, Moses did not stand for it. He would not allow himself to be treated in this way. In the end Moses arranged a contest between Korah and himself, which Korah lost. The lesson is that humility does not demand allowing others to walk all over you and to disregard your goals; it does, however, mean not perpetuating a fight just for the sake of self-importance and ego.

INSIGHT FOR BUSINESS: *When in a position of power, model your behavior after Moses: be aware of your strengths and your skills, but never use them for purely selfish goals and always be open-minded to good advice, regardless of its source. This does not mean that you should allow others to take control—be yourself and allow your own opinion to be important. Becoming a doormat is not a sign of humility; it is a sign of weakness.*

INSIGHT FOR LIFE: *Do not let arrogance or ego ruin your personal relationships, either. Remember Moses loved and revered his father-in-law, even though they bitterly disagreed, and even when Moses was in a position of such great power that nobody would have objected if he mistreated his father-in-law.*

Meditation

In this chapter, four different forms of self-representation have been discussed: the gas ruach *(person of coarse spirit), the* ba'al ga'ava *(the arrogant person), the humble person, and the doormat. Begin your meditation by thinking through each of these four categories, ensuring that you truly understand the personality type and actions each represents. When you feel that you have fully comprehended the four categories, the main part of the meditation can begin. Allow the idea of the* gas ruach *to flow through your mind. To help this repeat the words "gas ruach" over and over, each time thinking deeper about what it means and the type of personality it is. This should allow you to connect with it to the degree that you will become disgusted by the personality type.*

When this happens, meditate about whether you have any of the traits of the gas ruach. *If you can identify some (which would be normal) meditate about how this affects your business and your life. Connect with how the* gas ruach *aspect of your personality is ruinous for yourself and your business or career. This should motivate you to feel the need to change. Now it should be easy to decide to change the behavior pattern that is making you become a* gas ruach. *Do this often until you have broken the behavior pattern. The same type of meditation should be done for the* ba'al ga'ava *trait. Now think about humility and understand the Mosaic model of humility in all its depth. Once you feel that you have a full grasp of this, begin your meditation. Mediate about humility and how helpful it is for your business and your life. Allow the benefits of Mosaic humility to resonate with you on the deepest level. Then identify areas of your life where added humility is needed and as you realize how its increase can help you grow in business and make your life richer feel the surge of motivation to become humble. The same can be done for the doormat personality.*

CHAPTER 4

PATRIARCHAL BUSINESS MODELS
Creating a Blueprint for Success

In this way the man [Jacob] grew exceedingly prosperous and came to own large flocks, and maidservants and menservants, and camels and donkeys.

—GENESIS 30:43

CHANGING THE WORLD ISN'T EASY. Most of us find it difficult enough to change ourselves. While sometimes—in very rare cases—an individual man or woman makes the world a better place, it usually takes a group working together.

Several thousand years ago, three men changed the world. It began when Abraham realized that there was only one God who created and sustains the world. His son Isaac and his grandson Jacob carried on that belief to create a nation and a religion. It took them three generations, and their collective journey was filled with as many setbacks as successes. But just as a boy grows into a teen and then into a man, monotheism matured with these three patriarchs while their offspring—some of whom eventually became the Jewish nation—grew as well. This is all well documented in the Torah and its accompanying literature.

What is buried more deeply in the writings of the Torah is that the management philosophy of these three men grew in response to the challenges they faced. Abraham, it seems, tried to do everything himself without delegating his authority. And though Isaac was a master of delegation, he did not execute his vision into action—trusting that others would do that well enough. Jacob found the happy medium between those two styles, and thanks to the lessons learned from his father and grandfather, he completed the foundations of a religion that were so solid they have withstood several thousand years of strife.

To illustrate the lessons about leadership and business that can be learned from the three patriarchs, we have chosen examples from the telecommunications industry over the last decade. Just a few decades ago, telecommunications was a state-sanctioned monopoly. The business has endured years of wrenching technological and regulatory challenges, and clever leadership during this time period was at a premium. By perusing the pages of the recent business press, we can see reflections of the book of Genesis, which is where our story begins.

Smashing the Competition

One midrash (Bereishit Rabbah 38:13) tells the story of the boy Abraham in his father's shop, doing a little quality control. Abraham's father, Terach, sold idols to the people of Mesopotamia, part of what is today's Iraq. Townspeople relied on Terach to sell them the most powerful idols—those more mighty than the idols of their neighbors. Having a strong idol on your side was the Mesopotamia-dweller's version of having the nicest car on the block; not only did they believe it would ward off evil, but it could invoke envy in the eyes of kinsmen and colleagues.

Terach, like any good businessman, created multiple streams of revenue from his shop. Not only did he sell idols, he leased them, too. Customers could bring a sacrificial offering and, for a small fee, present it to one of the idols in the store. One day Terach left Abraham in charge while he attended to some business. This was a risky thing to do, because Abraham already had a nasty habit of mocking the shop's customers for believing in such superstitious nonsense.

But reading between the lines of this story, Abraham appears skeptical, questioning, and scientific in his approach to determining truths, as well as precocious in his dealings with his elders. And he's clearly unconcerned about sacrificing sales for the true prize. Abraham, in fact, is a master salesman. He's just not selling what his father would like him to be selling.

A woman walked into the shop, with a large plate of prepared food. "For me?" Abraham asked, not so innocently.

The woman frowned at him and ordered Abraham to place the plate in front of her favorite idol—which happened to be the smallest one in the shop. She paid her fee and left Abraham alone with the food and idols.

Then Abraham executed his plan. He took his father's axe and smashed all the idols in the room—except for the largest one. Then he placed the food tray in front of it and waited for his father to return.

In the evening, Terach arrived to see his entire store in disarray. Broken arms and legs littered the floor and the dust still hung in the air. He asked his son what on earth had happened to his expensive idols. "Well," Abraham replied, "a lady came in and offered a large plate of food to one of the smaller idols and a larger one wanted it, so he snatched it from him, and then an even bigger idol took it from that one, and before I knew it a great fight had broken out amongst all the idols in the store."

"Eventually," Abraham breathlessly explained to his father, "the biggest idol in the store got up and with an axe in his hands destroyed all of the other idols and then took the food for himself." And sure enough there, in the middle of the room, stood the only remaining idol—the tallest one—with the plate of delicacies at his feet and an axe at his side.

As any father with a precocious offspring can understand, Terach was not amused. "Do you take me for a fool," he thundered at his son. "I know that these idols can't move. They are just pieces of wood and stone. They can't eat food and they cannot fight!"

"So if they have no power," Abraham responded in a childlike tone, "why do you serve them?" However angry Terach might have been at the time, he would eventually agree with his son and become one of his first converts to monotheism.

Abraham's entire strategy here was risky, and the danger of angering his father was the least of that risk. Abraham lived in a country where idolatry was the state religion. In fact, Nimrod, who was the king at the time, saw himself as a deity and had idols representing himself made, which his subjects worshipped. So Abraham's actions were, in effect, an affront to the King. According to the midrash, Abraham was charged with that crime and sentenced to death. Abraham was given the choice of publicly bowing to idols or being thrown into a fiery furnace.

But keep in mind that he did not destroy his father's work out of folly. He had to have been deeply motivated to commit such an outrageous and risky act. Something compelled him to deviate from the norm, hurt his beloved father, and commit a treason that was punishable by death.

Nothing ever happens by chance. It's no coincidence that Abraham was born into a family of shopkeepers, the ancient world's version of the modern entrepreneur. Abraham would have been taught at an early age how to do a good sales job, how to deal with customers, how to manage books, and how to set prices high enough to make a profit but low enough to avoid being outcompeted. The son of a small businessman, raised in the marketplace and trained to make the sale, Abraham was driven by the same thing that drives most businessmen: he had something better to sell—a new, more powerful God that promised greater rewards than any wood and stone idol ever could.

This story sets the scene for the emergence of monotheism into the world. Young Abraham's belief in monotheism was so strong that he refused to bow to idols. Abraham kept steadfast to his monotheistic and anti-idolatry views, even as he faced certain death when King Nimrod had him thrown into the furnace. Tradition has it that he was miraculously untouched by the flames.

Abraham's public relations stunt with his father's idols succeeded even better than he could have imagined, earning him credibility and a reputation throughout Mesopotamia as an iconoclast and a holy man. All he had to do at this point was to build a religion using his effective advance marketing as a springboard. But Abraham's tactics did not immediately lead to the ultimate success he sought.

INSIGHT FOR BUSINESS: *Marketing is very important in any business, as is your credibility, sincerity, and belief in the product being sold. Bear in mind, however, that other ingredients are needed for sustained, long-term success.*

INSIGHT FOR LIFE: *Do what is right because it is right and not because it will bring you fame or money. Have the courage of your convictions to be different. Do not allow the influence of the prevailing culture cause you to forsake your values. Remember the importance of being credible in everything you do.*

Grassroots in the Desert: From the Bottom to the Top

Abraham wanted to build a successful brand. He wanted to bring new worshippers to the concept of a single God and make them understand God's power and glory and the importance of striving to be close to him. The midrash (Bereishit Rabbah 48:9) adds the following vital details about Abraham's business model. It tells how, after fleeing Nimrod's fury, he set up shop in the desert outside of Mesopotamia at a busy junction of trading paths. He built a large tent with four doors on each side and invited any passing traveler inside. Abraham would serve free meals to anyone who dropped in (Bereishit Rabbah 54:6). And while the traveler was eating, Abraham would preach to him about monotheism and God.

If Abraham was looking for quantity, his strategy worked. Despite the economic drain of providing so much free food, he was attracting thousands of converts who were excited about this new vision of the world and the new lifestyle and values that Abraham preached. They left his tent denouncing their previous idolatry and proclaiming praise for God. Further, they were enthusiastic about spreading the word to the world beyond.

But a careful reading of the Torah narrative and the midrash's commentaries shows that Abraham's success did not have the desired permanence. His main outreach was the tent in the desert. When the newly religious travelers made their way home, they found it difficult to maintain their excitement in the new faith. Their family members continued to worship idols and disregarded pleas to stop. Soon the travelers' willpower faded and they too went back to a polytheistic worldview. Abraham's thousands of converts turned into only a few sturdy followers, most of whom were his own family members. Why were Abraham's converts unable to remain loyal to his teachings over the long term?

A modern marketing consultant would conclude that Abraham's

converts did not remain loyal to his ideology because he didn't provide enough customer service infrastructure beyond the tent in the desert. Abraham had done a spectacular job of advertising and creating credibility, but he hadn't created the social system and the network of support that a religion needs to thrive. The Jewish mystical teachers, known as the Kabbalists, explain that Abraham's strategy was what they term "*milmatah lemalah*," or "from below to above." In other words, it was a grassroots strategy. Creating a successful religion however—like creating a new business—must include elements that will enhance customer satisfaction. Customer/devotee loyalty must be created. It's about creating a series of support systems, so that the customers become comfortable and trusting enough to remain loyal patrons.

Abraham, it seems, did not implement that middle section of the customer-care infrastructure. He cared very much about the customer/devotee, but his time and resources were completely dedicated to that one-on-one relationship between himself and the person he was teaching. He did not build a big organization. He created numerous individual followers who enthusiastically embraced his style of monotheism, but then had no community to become a part of. Abraham felt, it seems, that by virtue of his interaction with the individual he would be able to create something lasting.

Ultimately, however, he was unable to achieve customer/devotee loyalty. Instead, Abraham built a very small permanent following that, only with the work of his son and grandson (Isaac and Jacob), became a long-lasting success. No matter how much of a spectacular salesman Abraham was (and he must have been if he was able to sell monotheism to his father, who was making a nice business from polytheism), he did not create a huge organization that met the numerous needs of his thousands of followers. To do that, Abraham would have needed to delegate some of his responsibilities to others so that there would be more resources to cater to the needs of his new converts. This lack of delegation meant that he did not have the resources or manpower to create a backup community for the converts after they left his immediate sphere of influence.

Poor Follow-up Customer Care at Vonage

A present-day example of a company that followed in Abraham's footsteps in not delegating enough resources to provide a fulfilling post-sale experience for the customer is Vonage. This pioneer of Internet telephony was one of the first to market telephone service that used the Internet as its network instead of phone lines erected by the telephone company. Called Voice-Over-Internet-Protocol (VOIP), the emerging technology allowed new entrants into the field of telecommunications.

In the early years of the technology, Vonage quickly became the market leader. Its aggressive pricing and its elaborate marketing campaigns attracted millions of individuals and small businesspeople to choose its service over dozens of other start-ups. By 2005, it had accumulated more than 1.3 million paying VOIP subscribers—more than half of the entire market, which itself was expected to double in the next two years.

Yet just one year later, Vonage's IPO was in trouble and investors were selling their shares in the company. When the company finally held its IPO in May of 2006, it sold its shares to the market for only about one-fourth of what analysts had expected just a few months earlier. At the time of this writing, just two years after the IPO, the stock had lost more than 85 percent of its value.

What went wrong? Vonage, like Abraham, focused on that initial sale and failed to dedicate enough resources to build an elaborate customer support system. In February of 2006 the company admitted that it was spending more than $200 on advertising for each subscriber it had. That meant it would take at least a year to pay back the advertising cost from a new client's payments—a low return on investment unheard of in the world of marketing.

Vonage's choice to spend less on customer service than on advertising led to its reputation as a poor phone company. Calls were dropped, lines went dead, and static was too often heard. As a result, the company suffered a high rate of customer loss. Vonage may have been able to attract customers through their sophisticated marketing, but they did not put the infrastructure in place to achieve long-lasting customer loyalty.

Like Abraham, the Vonage executives thought they could build a business from the bottom to the top, only to find that it took a lot more expense and work to make people stick with the choice they had made. And like Abraham they have so far been unable to build a mighty entity. By the spring of 2008, executives were still warning investors that the company was on the brink of bankruptcy and were desperately looking to refinance their debt.

Vonage, like Abraham, was unable to give the customer an entire experience beyond the immediate service they were offering. In both cases there was no customer follow-up. The reasons were similar, too. Vonage put all its efforts into attracting the customer, but then did not have enough resources for adequate customer service. Abraham was the main principal of the new religion he had created, and instead of spreading his resources evenly, he used all his limited manpower to attract new converts. He did not leave enough time, energy, or manpower to create an infrastructure that new converts could fall back on.

Both Vonage and Abraham would have done well to assign some of their resources to enhancing customer service, so that the customer or devotee would have a wholesome experience and would thus remain loyal. Many small businesses fail as a result of an inability to allocate enough resources to customer service and thus ensure customer loyalty. While in the case of Vonage the lack of customer service was due to their belief that it was not necessary, in Abraham's case it was because of his hands-on business model where he, as CEO, managed everything and delegated almost nothing. The small businessperson must accept the fact that one person can't do it all. Delegation of responsibilities and resources evenly allows for business growth because the company is able to cater to each customer in many ways. There is only a limited amount one person can do in a twenty-four-hour period. The hands-on strategy will stifle the growth of an entrepreneurial organization because one person can only cater to a limited number of customers.

> INSIGHT FOR BUSINESS: *You and your family alone cannot grow a business to any significant size. As your business grows you cannot properly attend to the customer's/client's long-term needs on your own, thus giving them no reason to be loyal to you. Creating loyalty is as important for growth as attractive and innovative marketing.*

> INSIGHT FOR LIFE: *"The work is not for you to complete but neither are you permitted to desist from it," as we learn from the great Jewish text, Ethics of the Fathers. Don't ever think that you must do everything alone. Allow others to help you. Involve your friends and family in your goals and dreams.*

A New Paradigm Appears: From the Top to the Bottom

According to the following story from the Torah (Genesis 18:3–8) even at the age of ninety-nine Abraham was trying to keep tight control over everything. Three days after he had undergone a painful circumcision at the behest of God, three angels, disguised as humans appeared at Abraham's tent; he, Sarah, and his young son Ishmael were the ones who baked them bread and cooked them a meal. By this time he was wealthy enough to afford servants and food preparers. Yet this frail ninety-nine-year-old man and his equally aged wife continued to perform these tasks on their own. It's no wonder that his fledgling religion did not grow beyond a few hundred die-hard followers.

But the angels who visited him were there to tell him of the impending birth of his newest "employee"—his son Isaac. Abraham would now have a son to whom it would be suitable to pass on his legacy and who would do things differently. As Isaac grew up and observed his father's management style, he determined what needed to be done to expand the enterprise. Unlike his father who managed, as the Kabbalists say, *"milmatah lemalah"* (from the bottom to the top), Isaac operated *"milmalah lematah"* (from the top to the bottom): he surveyed a problem, initiated a solution, and then let others execute it—his was a hands-off approach. One example of this is that when it came time for Isaac to marry, he delegated the search for a spouse to a servant. He trusted that servant to make the wise decision of finding him a fitting wife.

Another illustration of this is the fact that it's mentioned in the Torah (Genesis 26:18) that Isaac would dig wells. The Torah commentators thus gave Isaac a nickname: the Well-Digger. Wells are actually just holes in the ground that allow natural spring water to burst forth under its own pressure. Once a spring had been identified, he would dig a well that would then supply water on its own for years to come. Wells need little maintenance after they have first been dug. This is significant because it gives us insight into his business model. Like his well digging, Isaac would start enterprises, put the right people in place, and then let them grow on their own, offering little or no input.

Probably the most well-known example of Isaac's *milmalah lematah,* his hands-off management approach, is the famous "trickster" scene from the Torah (Genesis 27:6–29), where Isaac's son Jacob seemingly tricked his father into bequeathing to him the coveted "firstborn" blessing that was meant for his twin brother Esau.

By the tribal conventions of the time, the birthright was naturally Esau's, as he emerged from the womb first. However, Esau had traded his birthright for a bowl of lentils. In addition, Esau showed none of Jacob's positive qualities. The Torah's narrative clearly favors Jacob as one who earned the birthright.

Isaac did not recognize this. He had decided at their birth that Esau would be his primary heir and that was that. He seemed unaware of Jacob's superior leadership skills and Esau's significant character flaws.

Jacob's mother Rebecca had a plan (Genesis 27:6–13). She told Jacob to go into Isaac's tent wearing a goat pelt and request his father's blessing. When Isaac, whose vision was failing at this point, reached out to touch his son, he felt the hair on his arm and assumed it was Esau, who was very hairy. This convinced Isaac to give Jacob the coveted firstborn blessings.

In Torah teachings, Jacob did what was necessary in order to gain what was in the best interest of the tribe, which would go on to become the Jewish nation. Rather than being a trickster who stole something that wasn't his, he is viewed by the tradition as being a clever tactician who prevented what would have been a calamity for his heirs.

On the other hand, although Isaac was a master of delegating tasks and initiating enterprises, his overly hands-off management style had certain drawbacks. As a consequence of this hands-off leadership style, if not for the quick wit of his wife and younger son he would have bestowed the choice firstborn blessings upon the wicked Esau.

A Lack of Vision at MCI

Bernie Ebbers is a prime example of the potential effects of an overly hands-off leadership style. As one of the mighty Wall Street icons of the Internet boom, when the chips were down, he led his company to ruin. That company was MCI Worldcom, one of the major long distance providers in the late 1990s. Providing long distance service was a dying business; new technologies were turning it into a low-profit-margin, declining-revenue industry.

Ebbers took MCI Worldcom's vast capital resources and began buying up local telephone companies throughout the country. His acquisition pace was so rapid that MCI Worldcom seemed to be adding a new purchase every month. Even MCI Worldcom's large cash reserves could not sustain the practice, so Ebbers turned to Wall Street lenders, who provided him with leveraged debt to increase their return on investment. By 1999, Ebbers was famous for turning a dying company into a high-growth juggernaut. This one-time high school basketball coach had become a self-made billionaire.

It would not last long. When the market fell in 2001, Ebbers's "roll-up" strategy backfired. MCI Worldcom's stock declined rapidly and its massive debts started coming due. The company was overleveraged and undercapitalized. By 2002, MCI Worldcom was bankrupt, Ebbers was fired, and investors had lost a stunning $180 billion.

But the worst was yet to come for Ebbers. Criminal charges of accounting fraud were filed against him and his fellow executives. His defense consisted of a "Who, little old me?" tactic. Ebbers told the jury that while his subordinates were engaging in fraud, he was incapable of understanding the complex accounting schemes they presented to him. "I'm just a physical education major," he famously pleaded from the stand.

If Ebbers was telling the truth and hadn't engaged directly in fraud, he was still guilty of poor leadership. Ebbers's self-described hands-off style of management, with its lack of proper oversight, led his company to disaster. Today, Bernie Ebbers sits in a Louisiana jail cell and will not be eligible for parole until 2028.

> **INSIGHT FOR BUSINESS:** *Once a business or project is up and running, there is often a temptation to pull away and allow it to run on its own. Resist this urge and remain involved. Continue with detailed oversight. Remember, an overly hands-off approach to management may not end well.*

> **INSIGHT FOR LIFE:** *Everything in life needs active work if it is to continue succeeding. Relationships need constant care. You cannot just get married and then neglect the relationship, assuming that it will continue to thrive on its own.*

Jacob Gets It Just Right

So if Abraham's hands-on strategy was incomplete and Isaac's hands-off strategy had drawbacks, how did Jacob find success? It's little surprise that Jacob is revered by tradition as a model for effective leadership. It's also no revelation that Jacob's key to success was finding the proper balance between the two management styles. Jacob did not reject his father's or his grandfather's wisdom. Instead he combined them into a far more powerful mode of leadership.

To illustrate this, let's return to the Torah's narrative where we left off (Genesis 29). When Esau heard that his brother had taken the firstborn blessings, he planned to kill him. Jacob fled from the land of Canaan and spent the next number of years in the house of Laban, his uncle, working for him. Laban was known as a swindler. In fact, Laban's dishonesty was so great that he even cheated Jacob out of his promised bride. Laban had two daughters: Rachel and

Leah. Jacob had fallen in love with Rachel and made a deal with Laban that he would work seven years for him if thereafter he was given Rachel as a wife.

But Laban tricked Jacob. When he awoke the morning after the wedding, Jacob discovered that he had married Leah and not Rachel. This was possible in a time when women were veiled during the wedding ceremony. (To this day, at Jewish wedding ceremonies the groom himself places the veil on the bride before the wedding ceremony begins, thus ensuring that Jacob's heirs do not fall into the same trap that he did.) Laban had deceived Jacob and given him the wrong woman to marry. Laban then demanded that he work an additional seven years if he wanted to marry Rachel as well. Now remember that Laban was also Jacob's main business partner, and it was in this type of environment that Jacob had to grow his enterprise. Against all odds, Jacob's agricultural business flourished, and by the end of the second seven-year period he had become even wealthier than Laban.

But how was Jacob able to prosper financially in such a difficult business environment? The Torah gives the answer and other ancient texts expound on it. According to the Torah, Jacob worked harder than anyone else in Laban's encampment (Genesis 31:40): "I was [in the field] by day when the heat consumed me, and the frost at night, and my sleep wandered from my eyes." Jacob knew that if he turned away from his work for even a moment he would be deceived out of his money. He was constantly vigilant and built his fortune through sweat and pain.

Contrast that style of work with a hands-off management style where the boss initiates projects and then removes him- or herself from their execution. Jacob, who it can be inferred from the Torah's narrative had a number of workers whom he supervised, both initiated and delegated. He also was involved in the hard practical work of agricultural production. This balanced management style, no doubt, contributed greatly to his massive success.

INSIGHT FOR BUSINESS: *There is no substitute for old-fashioned hard work. But in addition to working hard you must work smart and ensure that the correct energies and resources are directed to where they are most needed. This includes having proper knowledge and supervision of all areas of the business, especially those that can be problematic.*

INSIGHT FOR LIFE: *Realize that even the people closest to you can have their own best interest at heart rather than yours. Safeguard yourself from being manipulated by others. Although advice from friends and family is important to consider, in the final analysis you are on your own. As the sages said: "If I am not for myself who is for me? But if I am only for myself what am I?" (Ethics of the Fathers 114) The balance between looking out for self and caring for others is vital for a successful life.*

Knowing the Business Better Than Your Competition

Another hallmark of Jacob's balance between the hands-on and hands-off business approach was his ability to thrive in adverse circumstances by having a detailed and ever growing understanding of his businesses mechanisms and technology. When faced with his uncle's trickery and the potential loss of the love of his life, Jacob adapted Laban's game and then played it better than his uncle.

He did this by making an odd offer to Laban (Genesis 30). Instead of being paid his portion of the profits in cash, Jacob requested that he get every speckled baby goat and every brown lamb that was to be born to the family herd. Not understanding Jacob's plan and mistakenly thinking that the deal would benefit him most, Laban jumped at the offer. Then, sneaking behind Jacob's back, he secretly removed all the speckled goats and brown sheep from the flock, ensuring that Jacob received nothing for all his hard work.

This is where the Torah's narrative takes an odd twist. Jacob fashioned wooden sticks with bark stripped from them so that they had striped patterns. The goats that mated near these sticks then had speckled offspring. Likewise, the sheep that mated near the striped sticks gave birth to brown lambs. In its typical literary sparseness and economy of words, the Torah does not explain why this trick worked. Perhaps it was the supernatural intervention of God. Or perhaps the peeled wood emitted some chemical compound that caused a mutation. Or perhaps a certain type of livestock that had a recessive gene for speckled or brown offspring was attracted to the striped sticks.

Whatever the reason, the source of Jacob's cleverness is clear: his intimate knowledge of animal husbandry earned through many years of working closely with his herds. He knew something about livestock breeding that Laban did not and he exploited that information to earn a vast fortune. He turned Laban's greed to his own advantage and, without lying or committing any sin, became fabulously wealthy. This is indicative of Jacob's balanced approach to business management. He was an expert in every aspect of his business and did not leave others to learn the intricacies of animal breeding; as CEO he knew that *he* had to have all the cutting edge knowledge available to succeed.

There is an additional modern-day analogy that can be gleaned from this Biblical story as well. Jacob's striped sticks were, essentially, a new and advanced technology. Jacob understood that technology better than Laban did and used that knowledge to his advantage. One of the modern business executive's foremost obligations is to understand the intricacies of new technologies in his or her field and to be able to strategize a way for the company to benefit—and not get damaged—by those changes.

INSIGHT FOR BUSINESS: *The ability to understand the ever-changing business environment and adapt to new circumstances is vital for success in business. This was the case thousands of years ago when things changed very slowly and is certainly the case in our fast-moving world. Never delegate the learning of new technologies and business mechanisms vital for your business to others. In order to compete, you need to make educated decisions that are right for your particular field.*

INSIGHT FOR LIFE: *Life situations change. Love matures over time, as do relationships. Often you have ups and downs in your personal and financial circumstances. You must learn to adapt to new situations and circumstances quickly.*

Executing Jacob's Vision Today: Howard Jonas and IDT

There's a very wealthy Bronx native named Howard Jonas who serves as a modern-day example of someone who followed in Jacob's footsteps. Jonas founded a company called IDT (International Discount Telecommunications) Corp., in 1992 after learning about a new telecommunications technology called international call-back. This system allowed a person in a foreign country, where calls to the United States were as much as $5 a minute at the time, to reroute their U.S.-bound call as if it were originating in the United States (where international calls were less than $1 a minute).

His company very quickly grew into a telecommunications powerhouse worth tens of millions of dollars a year. But it wasn't until AT&T sued him, claiming his technology was illegal, that he garnered fame. Jonas had done his homework. The call-back system took advantage of a loophole in international telecommunications treaties, but was perfectly legal—and he won the lawsuit.

By the late 1990s, Jonas invested in Voice-Over-Internet-Protocol by founding a company called Net2Phone. In 2001, at the very climax of the dot-com boom, he sold the company to AT&T for $1.1 billion. One year later, amidst the ashes of the telecom market collapse, Jonas bought the company back for a mere $100 million. He then spent most of the rest of his $1 billion on buying up the equipment of other bankrupt telecommunications providers at fire sale prices. Today, IDT is one of the thousand largest companies in the world—not bad considering it did not even exist twenty years ago.

Perhaps Jonas is one of the luckiest men in the world. Perhaps he just happened to buy at the lowest possible moment and sell at the highest possible moment because of a roll of the cosmic dice. But the fact that he did so several times in his career (and there's plenty more career in his future—he is only fifty years old) points to an unusually deep understanding, like Jacob's, of his industry, its technologies, and the laws that affect it. He started IDT and was its sole employee for its first year. And like Jacob he always involved himself deeply in the daily operations of his company, while keeping his eye on the wider business landscape to make wise strategic decisions. And Jonas also understood new technologies and the impacts they would have better than his rivals—indicating a strong participation in all aspects of his company's operation. In other words, like Jacob, he practiced a synthesis of a top-down and bottom-up, hands-on and hands-off, business strategy.

Jacob's True Legacy

After his time with Laban, Jacob still had a challenge. After becoming wealthy while working for his father-in-law, Jacob was finally freed from his servitude. The world lay before him, full of business opportunities.

But in addition to continuing his successful sheep-herding business, Jacob also concentrated on finishing the work started by his father and grandfather: building the new religion. Jacob's greatest contribution to Judaism (and by extension to world history) was not only through the work he did personally. It was also through the effort of his twelve sons, each of whom propagated a new tribe—the twelve tribes of Israel.

But Jacob chose the path of intense involvement in his sons' education and guidance. A large section of the end of the book of Genesis describes his deathbed speech to his sons, giving them advice and wisdom to carry on the nation and the new faith.

The vast impact that the Torah and its teachings have had on the world would never have happened had it not been for the religion's three patriarchs, Abraham, Isaac, and Jacob. Each was a deeply holy man, and each is revered for his contributions to the founding of the people and the religion. While Abraham and Isaac suffered setbacks during their primacy, Jacob's leadership was the culmination of the efforts of three generations to realize a dream. As a group they succeeded, just as God had told them they would.

Reading the Torah's story of these three great men, along with the accompanying commentaries, it's important to appreciate each of the men for his own strengths. We can all judge ourselves against these ancient prototypes. And we can strive to find, as Jacob did, the perfect balance between a "top-to-bottom" or hands on and "bottom-to-top" or hands off approach. Once you have mastered the balance between the two, you are well on the way to running a successful enterprise.

INSIGHT FOR BUSINESS: *Make sure you understand the business environment in which you are working, from the lowliest job to the most complex one. You don't need to be able to do every task, but you must understand everything that happens inside the or-*

ganization. While it is important to delegate responsibilities, never abdicate supervision. It is important that you keep tabs on the entire process from top to bottom and from bottom to top.

INSIGHT FOR LIFE: *Keep all aspects of your life in balance. Extremes in any direction lead to setbacks in another. Make sure to be involved in your own life by not allowing decisions to be made for you by others—but at the same time, take the opinions of friends and family seriously.*

Meditation

This chapter is about getting the correct managerial and leadership balance for your business. Think about your business and figure out whether you have the right balance between hands-off and hands-on management. Are you too controlling? Or are you too hands-off and withdrawn? Determine which aspect you need to change. Then meditate on the words "I must find the right managerial and leadership balance." If you are too controlling, then add in the words "I must be more hands-off" to your meditation. If you need to supervise more, then add the words "I must be more hands-on" to your meditation. As you are thinking of these words, allow your mind to think about your business and how a lack of the right balance is harming it. Allow the feeling of the harm your current approach is doing to deeply resonate with you. Connect to that feeling. Now think about whether delegating tasks and responsibilities, or providing greater guidance and supervision, would make your business more successful. Whichever one it is allow that conclusion to linger—connect to it. This way you will feel motivated to make the necessary changes in your business and life. Use the guide in the Appendix to help you with this meditation.

CHAPTER 5

MAKING THE SALE
Negotiation Techniques from the Torah

If there are ten as you say I will save them on account of the ten.

—GOD TO ABRAHAM IN GENESIS

NEGOTIATING AFFECTS ALMOST EVERY ASPECT OF OUR LIVES. We are social beings who require interaction with other people. Since no two people think alike or have exactly the same desires, we constantly have to negotiate with others about all sorts of things. In fact, we often do not realize that we are negotiating with our spouses, family, friends, or colleagues. We just think it is part of everyday conversation. In business, negotiation often takes on an official appearance—people sit around a boardroom table on opposite sides and speak in serious and deliberate sentences, trying to get the best deal. No doubt the skills we can learn about negotiations in the boardroom can help us everywhere else as well.

Negotiation is the process that takes place when two parties with different needs but similar aims meet to reach their individual aspirations while showing respect for the other's needs. If there is a lack of respect for the wishes of the other party, the negotiations will fail. To ensure mutual success and to guarantee that the deal is closed, smart negotiation tactics should be followed. Unsurprisingly, the Torah has tremendous insights into effective negotiation tactics that will help us in all of our interactions with others. Negotiations need not be painful or filled with dread if we understand how to handle them properly.

In the Torah we find humans negotiating intensely with God. Lives were at stake and the person negotiating with God felt an urgency to succeed. In one example, to be examined below, God's mind was changed and the people were saved. In another, the negotiation tactic didn't save lives but succeeded in its objectives nonetheless.

In addition, we find characters from the Torah negotiating with each other. Jacob negotiated with other humans over important issues such as his choice of spouse, his business contract for fourteen years, and his birthright and privileges. By analyzing the negotiations and tactics found in the Torah we can gain insight into effective negotiating techniques that are as applicable in today's boardrooms as they were thousands of years ago at the top of Mt. Sinai.

INSIGHT FOR BUSINESS: *Realize that you are negotiating even when you don't consciously recognize it, and that negotiating skills are needed for every aspect of business life. The more you hone your negotiating skills, the more success you will have in business.*

INSIGHT FOR LIFE: *When you talk with your friends you are negotiating. When you go out on a date you are negotiating. Negotiations are a necessary part of human interactions and most of them you do effortlessly. The instances that can lead to serious and heated arguments or a falling out with others require more advanced negotiating skills.*

Abraham Negotiates with God

The Torah relates the story of the two cities, Sodom and Gomorrah, whose people were exceptionally wicked. According to the midrash (Bereishit Rabbah 41:8), both places were filled with immoral and murderous inhabitants. Hospitality, for example, was prohibited in Sodom and Gomorrah and was punishable by a cruel death. In addition, extreme sexual immorality was pervasive.

God decided that He was going to destroy the inhabitants of Sodom and Gomorrah and informed Abraham of his decision. Abraham objected to God killing thousands of people, the righteous together with the wicked, and he began negotiating a peaceful settlement. Abraham used a number of negotiating tactics for this. He used questions that would shed doubt on the reasons for destroying Sodom and Gomorrah. He asked God if justice would be served if he were to kill the righteous together with the wicked. He also used a different approach suggesting to God that there might be fifty righteous people in Sodom and Gomorrah. He then followed up with another question, asking if it was becoming for God to perform collective punishment and kill them rather than forgive all the inhabitants on account of the potentially fifty righteous people in the cities. Abraham further asked God whether it is possible that God as the judge of the entire earth can do something that is unjust. God replies that He would not destroy Sodom and Gomorrah if there were, in fact, fifty righteous people living there.

The problem, however, was that fifty righteous people were not to be found. Abraham persisted, and asked whether God would save the city if there were forty-five righteous inhabitants, and again forty-five righteous people could not be found. Eventually Abraham achieved a final concession from God that if even ten could be found He would not destroy Sodom and Gomorrah in their merit. But even ten could not be found. With this the fate of Sodom and Gomorrah was sealed and were set to be destroyed the following day.

An analysis of Abraham's negotiations shows that he tried a two-pronged approach with the use of questions being a primary tactic. First, he challenged the concept and justice of collective punishment. Second, he suggested that there were numerous righteous people in Sodom and Gomorrah. What Abraham was in fact saying—the sages say—is that since the flood (where God destroyed the entire population of earth except for Noah and his family), there had been a perception that God kills righteous and wicked together indiscriminately.

Through the clever use of questions, Abraham was hinting to God that, if there were righteous people there, killing everyone in Sodom and Gomorrah (including righteous people) would be a massive public relations blunder that would damage God's reputation. Ultimately, these arguments were rejected by the facts: there were not even ten righteous people in Sodom and Gomorrah.

The fact that ten righteous people couldn't be found meant that the overwhelming majority of the inhabitants of the two cities were wicked and therefore liable for punishment. By negotiating, Abraham had given God the opportunity to say that if there were righteous people in Sodom and Gomorrah He would have saved the entire population of extremely evil people on account of them. Although in this case Abraham was unable to save Sodom and Gomorrah, he achieved his aim, which was to ensure that justice was being performed and that good people were not being punished on account of their wicked neighbors.

We may conclude that Abraham was employing a strategy of not negotiating on the price (the destruction of Sodom and Gomorrah) but rather on a condition (establishment of a precedent for the dispensation of justice). In other words, he did not go for broke, asking God to completely repeal His decision to destroy Sodom and Gomorrah. Instead, he questioned a side idea, which was the justice of killing the righteous with the wicked. This bought Abraham some real bargaining leverage. He was now able to search for some righteous people: If he found them, he would be able to negotiate a hold on the pending destruction. The fact that Abraham couldn't find righteous people was beside the point, because he nonetheless won the negotiations. God got what He wanted, which was the destruction of the cities. Abraham got what he wanted, which was to see that real justice had been carried out so that the righteous were not punished on the account of the wicked.

In business, this strategy is instructive. In a deal where the other party seems to have made up their mind and has a strong position, it is always important to take Abraham's lead and not confront them head on. Try to look for an area other than price that could lead to a successful outcome. Look at the terms and conditions of the deal where, if a concession is made, it could significantly change the dynamics of the deal. However, the concession that is sought must be one that does not destroy the other party's position. This way a concession can be made that allows both parties to realize their goals.

Most deals involve side issues that can be negotiated and can affect the bottom line without being confrontational. When buying a house, for example, there is the price of the house and then there are other areas like furniture, repairs and upgrades, or financing. Negotiating over those side items can change the bottom line. And even if it does not, concessions can still be made without significantly changing the dynamics of the deal, leading to a successful negotiation.

Southwestern Production Corporation: Negotiating over Terms and Conditions Rather Than Price

By 1992, after getting a master's degree in geology and working as a field geologist for a large natural gas company, Jim Williams was ready to start his own company.

One of the first projects of his new company, Southwestern Production Corporation, was the purchase of a large plot of gas fields near Durango, Colorado. The fields needed work, but they offered a rare perk: once the wells were modernized, they would have a very long production lifetime. For a company that had too many short-lifetime wells, the refurbished fields would be worth a lot of money. Williams also knew of other nearby plots that could be purchased. By incorporating the different plots into one large plot, he knew he could increase the value of the assets.

There was one problem. The owner of the largest plot was Mobil Corporation, one of the world's largest energy companies. Williams knew that the plot was not one of Mobil's core assets and he expected that they would potentially be happy to sell it. Sure enough, Mobil expressed interest in selling the land to Southwestern, but as things progressed it became increasingly difficult for Williams to get his phone calls returned by senior executives.

In preparation for the negotiations, however, Williams analyzed what he knew about Mobil. They appeared to be rock solid in their trustworthiness—if they said they were going to do something, they would do it. But their internal processes moved very slowly. Williams decided to take advantage of this fact in the negotiations. "You will rarely be able to budge someone from the price that they need to get," says Williams. "So you're usually better off demanding something in the terms or the conditions. If you are able to meet their price target, they won't let some innocuous statement deep in the contract stop them from completing the deal."

Thus, Williams decided on his negotiating strategy—he would not quibble over the price, which had already been agreed upon in general terms. And he would not press hard for any specific terms of the agreement. But he would slip a condition into the talks that the other side probably would not be particular about. He would stake his claim on that condition and make it a deal-killer if it weren't included in the final contract.

That condition was to set the date of sale to the point of first contact between the parties. Traditionally, in the oil and gas industry, deals are set into stone at the signing of the contract. But Williams could already see that the agreement would have to go through several layers of bureaucracy within Mobil, and that would take time. Consequently, he wanted to reap the profits from the gas production during that interim period between the handshake and the final, signed agreement.

Not surprisingly, the Mobil negotiators did not balk at his condition—they were happy to have avoided protracted negotiations over the dollar amount of the sale. And sure enough, the gears within Mobil churned very slowly. It took eight months before the final agreement was signed. That meant that Williams's company added eight months' worth of gas production to their balance sheet, amounting to several hundred thousand dollars. This, of course, considerably lessened the cost of purchasing the property, and while the price itself did not change, money was returned to Southwestern at closing. In the end Southwestern Production realized more than a 30 percent profit when they sold the site a few months later.

Jim Williams had correctly recognized that he could make more money with a favorable condition than if he had devoted all his resources towards getting a better price, just as Abraham realized his objective by concentrating on a condition (justice) rather than the price (the destruction of the cities).

INSIGHT FOR BUSINESS: *When negotiating, always look at the entire picture and realize that sometimes, by tackling the smaller issues, the larger ones will be affected and thus fall into place on their own.*

INSIGHT FOR LIFE: *Don't think that you can make major changes in people. Your business partner or spouse should not be seen as a project of yours to change. However, if you can negotiate some small changes in their behavior, it can make a big difference to your lives.*

Jacob Negotiates with His Brother

Another negotiation lesson we can learn from the Torah is the perfect win-win strategy. In the previous chapter we mentioned that Jacob traded a bowl of lentil soup for his older brother Esau's birthright. The story (Genesis 25:29–34) is that Esau came in from a day of hunting (and murdering, according to the midrash, Bereishit Rabbah 63:12) and wanted to eat. Jacob was preparing a pot of lentil soup and Esau asked for some. Jacob said, "Sell me your birthright," to which Esau replied that he had no need for the birthright and was therefore prepared to sell it to him in exchange for the soup. But before the transaction closed, Jacob made Esau swear that he had indeed sold the birthright. Esau swore and the deal was closed.

Here we find an example of a classic win-win strategy. A win-win negotiating scenario can best be achieved when the deal is between something that is important and valuable for one side but less significant and valuable for the other party. In this case, Esau did not see the birthright as important and, according to the commentaries (Rashi, Genesis 25:32), did not feel able to live up to its expectations. At that moment, however, the bowl of lentil soup was extremely important to him. Thus, he was happy to sell it. Jacob conversely could have easily cooked another pot of soup; but the birthright would guarantee him a special place in the family and later on unique blessings from his father Isaac. To Jacob, buying the birthright for a bowl of soup was a real bargain.

Citigroup: Anybody Want a Few Tons of Rock?

Scott Patten had dead weight on his hands, many tons of it, in fact. As an investment banker with Citigroup, he was charged with selling a successful California-based granite and marble distribution company.

The problem was that this company had recently begun a Colorado branch that had failed. While the failed Colorado venture was not part of the sale, the company still wanted to get rid of the more than $1.5 million worth of granite sitting in the Denver warehouse. Normally, when a business fails, its remaining inventory is sold by auction and shipped to the highest bidder. If this had been done in this case, the California company would have realized a major loss. Due to its weight and the expense of transporting it back to California, shipping the granite was not financially viable either. They therefore needed to continue paying to store it in Colorado until they were able to get rid of it some other way. The longer the rock lay in storage, the more its value was eaten up by the rental costs of the storage space.

Patten solved his client's problem using a classic win-win strategy. He found a national rock distributor with Denver operations who wanted to buy the California operation. He then crafted an offer that, in addition to buying the successful part of the company, called for the buying party to buy the $1.5 million of the granite housed in Denver and to pay half of the rent for housing it for a year and the selling party would pay the other half. Both parties also agreed that if the buyer was unable to use all the granite within a year of the closing of the deal, they would deduct the remaining amount from the price paid for the company.

In this instance, the Denver-based national distributor was like Jacob and the California-based granite company was like Esau. Just as Esau was happy to offload his birthright in exchange for soup, the California-based granite company needed to divest itself of the granite in exchange for money. And, just as Jacob wanted the birthright and was willing to pay for it, similarly the Denver-based national distributor needed granite in Denver and was willing to pay the market price to obtain it. In other words, each side had something that the other side needed but that was less valuable to them and therefore was happy to exchange it for something that was of more value to them. They both met and negotiated, and due to the circumstances in common ended with a win-win outcome.

> **INSIGHT FOR BUSINESS:** *Identify the true goal you want to achieve in the negotiations and then be flexible in finding a way to achieve it. Be creative in the manner in which you structure the agreement—the only important result is that you achieve your goal.*

> **INSIGHT FOR LIFE:** *In all of your relationships you have things to share with others that may mean a lot to them, but are easy for you to provide. Time is one of those things. It may mean a great deal to your loved ones if you spend more time with them, and for you it is something that, if made a priority, can be given without much compromise.*

Moses Understands God's Position

There is another successful negotiating tactic in the Torah: understanding the other side's position. Moses had ascended Mount Sinai to receive instructions from God and the two tablets of the covenant known in Hebrew as the *luchot habrit* (Exodus 31:18). Moses was supposed to have been away for forty days and forty nights. However, the Israelites miscalculated (Exodus 32:1–8) and on the fortieth day mistakenly thought that Moses had been killed and was not going to descend. The people therefore approached their high priest, Aaron, who was also Moses's brother, and told him that they wanted to create an idol in place of Moses who, they thought, had disappeared never to return.

Aaron reluctantly acquiesced to their request and told the Israelites to remove the golden jewelry and earrings from their wives and children and bring them to him. Aaron did this as a delaying tactic, hoping that the women would object to having their jewelry used for such profane purposes. However, the men did not give the women and children a chance to object. They took the earrings off their ears and snatched their jewelry, using force when necessary. Within a short period of time, enough gold was gathered to create an idol. Aaron took all the gold, fashioned a golden calf, and pronounced it the god of Israel who had brought them up from Egypt.

The next day, the people arose early and began offering up sacrifices to the golden calf. A pagan party then ensued which included such immoral behavior as incest and adultery. The Israelites had returned to the idolatry they had learned during their time of servitude in Egypt. At this point, God told Moses what was happening at the base of the mountain. He related to Moses how the Israelites had forsaken Him and built an idol which they were now worshiping and declaring as their god. And then He told Moses (Exodus 32: 9–10): "I have seen this people and they are a stiff-necked people. Now leave Me alone, and My anger will be kindled against them so that I will annihilate them, and I will make you into a great nation."

Upon hearing that God wanted to kill the entire nation of Israel, Moses began pleading for mercy on their behalf. Here, instead of saying that there were righteous people amongst the Israelites—which would have been correct—and pleading to God not to do something that was unjust as Abraham had done, Moses took a slightly different tack. Let us examine the exact words Moses used.

Moses pleaded before the Lord, his God, and said (Exodus 32:11-14):

> "Why, O Lord, should Your anger be kindled against Your people whom You have brought up from the land of Egypt with great power and with a strong hand? Why should the Egyptians say: 'He brought them out with evil intent to kill them in the mountains and to annihilate them from upon the face of the earth'? Retreat from the heat of Your anger and reconsider the evil intended for Your people. Remember Abraham, Isaac, and Israel, Your servants, to whom You swore by Your very Self, and to whom You said: 'I will multiply your seed like the stars of the heavens, and all this land which I said that I would give to your seed, they shall keep it as their possession forever.'" The Lord then reconsidered the evil He had said He would do to His people.

With this argument, Moses persuaded God to retreat from his previously stated decision to annihilate the Israelites and to begin anew with Moses and his descendents. An analysis of Moses's negotiating strategy shows that he did three things here: he used questions, he asked whether God's intent was in his best interests, and he asked whether it was in line with God's own policy.

The Use of Questions. First, Moses appeals to God's pride and asks God why He would expend such energy in taking the Israelites out of Egypt using unprecedented miracles only later to kill them. Moses was using questions to suggest that such action would show that God misjudged things and expended a "strong hand" for the wrong people. Notice how, like Abraham before him, Moses was using the negotiating technique of questioning to great effect.

Is It in Your Best Interests? Secondly, Moses tells God that killing the Israelites would not be in His own interests. The Egyptians were skeptical of God's powers anyway and were just looking for a way to say that this God who had defeated them was not so mighty after all. Moses was telling God that if he killed the Israelites, the Egyptians would say that the God of Israel had lost strength and could not finish the job of taking the Israelites into the Promised Land, and so, to save face, He killed them in the desert. This would diminish God's perceived power in the world. This strategy is very effective in all negotiations. If you can show the other party that their position is not in their own interests, succeeding in negotiations is far simpler.

Is It in Line with Your Own Policy? Moses's third strategy was to remind God of promises He had made to the Israelites' forefathers, Abraham, Isaac, and Jacob. He had said that their descendents would inherit the Promised Land and would become a numerous and great nation. Moses told God that if he were to kill the Israelites, He would be breaking those promises.

In other words, Moses neither confronted God nor questioned His justice or His omniscience. Instead, Moses made God realize that he was truly on His side. Moses made it known that he was looking out for God's interests. Moses was gently telling God that killing the Israelites would not get Him closer to His real goal: recognition in this physical world that is seemingly devoid of Divinity. Instead, it would bring ridicule upon God—the opposite of what God had really wanted to achieve when He emancipated the Israelites from Egypt. To negotiate in this way, Moses had to first have a very good understanding of what God really wanted and what was motivating His desire to kill the Israelites. Moses realized this when the

Israelites worshipped the golden calf. They had insulted God and caused His recognition to be diminished. This was counter to what God was aiming for. Moses then subtly explained to God that killing the Israelites would only further diminish that recognition and not take Him in the direction He wanted to go. Killing the Israelites would lesson God's status in the eyes of the Egyptians, the other nations, and even in the eyes of Moses, because He would have been breaking his pledge to Abraham, Isaac, and Jacob. Moses thus showed God how the act of killing the Israelites was against His own agenda. Moses' technique here was to really understand the other side's needs and then show them how they are able to reach them. This ended up being a winning technique.

So let's sum up. God wanted to kill the Israelites for sinning with the golden calf. Moses did not want that to happen. Now Moses needed to negotiate with God to ensure that the Israelites were not killed, but simultaneously he needed to calm God's anger. Moses came up with the perfect strategy: he showed God how, in fact, both of their aims coincided—Moses's desire that the Israelites be spared from death and God's longing for continued recognition. When this was proven clearly, God no longer had a reason to follow His previous plan.

This strategy also works in business negotiations. Although one side sometimes concedes to the other and capitulates almost one hundred percent, they nonetheless feel that they have succeeded as well. By asking the correct questions and making the right comments during the negotiations, the other party can be shown how their position is not beneficial to themselves. This is the best possible outcome. Sometimes, however, the other side has the ability to answer the questions and show how their position is better for them. If this happens, the negotiations may break down. But at least a confrontational argument does not ensue and relations are still strong enough for negotiations to continue on another deal on a different day.

This concept of knowing the other side's needs has been succinctly stated by Herb Cohen, author of the New York Times bestseller *You Can Negotiate Anything* (Bantam, 1982): "Successful collaborative negotiation lies in finding out what the other side really wants and showing them a way to get it while you get what you want." This is another one of the keys to successful negotiations that Moses understood thousands of years ago and students of the Torah have internalized and used for many millennia.

In addition to this, Moses was showing God that there was a better way forward. In negotiations, one should only continue negotiating if the negotiations will yield a result that is better than the Best Alternative to a Negotiated Agreement (BATNA). In this case, God's BATNA was to kill the Israelites. Moses was showing that a negotiated settlement would garner Him better results. This is instructive. Whenever you go into negotiations, you must make sure that what you have to offer is better than the BATNA of the other party. If it isn't, the negotiations will not succeed.

> **INSIGHT FOR BUSINESS:** *The key to winning a negotiation is knowledge—knowledge of yourself, knowledge of your negotiating partner, and knowledge of the fair value of the deal. With knowledge, a number of tactics can be used, such as asking questions, showing the other side how their position is out of sync with their own values and policies, or persuading the other side to come closer to your side through skillful arguments of what is in their best interests. Do your homework regarding the other party's situation, policies, and aims so that you can argue that a compromise benefiting you will benefit them as well.*

> **INSIGHT FOR LIFE:** *Try to get away from superficial assertions about others and instead reach deeper and endeavor to comprehend the other person's feelings and needs. On the level of feelings*

*and needs, all humans can relate to each other because we all
have similar feelings about things and our basic human needs are
also virtually the same. By grasping what is really going on with
the other person deep down, resolution to potential conflicts is
much more likely."*

Cerberus Capital: Solving the Other Side's Problems

One of the fiercest bidding wars in American corporate history
took place in the early months of 2007 over Chrysler Corporation.
The winner, Cerberus Capital, succeeded due to a creative negotiating strategy that ensured that all of the parties involved achieved
their goals. They were able to do this because they fully understood
the needs of all parties involved.

Cerberus was founded in the early 1990s by a group of Wall Street
veterans who wanted to not only own shares in companies, but to actually take over troubled companies, turn their operations around,
and then profit from the increased value of the company. The mech-
anism they created, the private equity fund, became very popular in
the early 2000's as billions of dollars in capital poured in.

Private equity firms have a fearsome reputation as plunderers willing to lay off thousands in order to ensure a return on their investments. Some do work that way, but not all. Cerberus, for instance,
successfully turned around many companies without massive layoffs
or long-term damage to the companies.

But that did not stop the founders of the firm from naming it after the three-headed hound that, according to Greek mythology,
guards the gates of hell. They wanted to use the terrifying stereotype
of their industry to their advantage in negotiations with competitors and labor unions. As one Chrysler union leader told *Portfolio*
magazine, "It's not a coincidence that they did not name it after a
cute little furry puppy."

When the executives at DaimlerChrysler announced in February of 2007 that their Chrysler unit was for sale, it surprised few observers of the automotive scene. Daimler, the parent company of Mercedes, had bought the struggling American carmaker in 1999 for $37 billion. All hailed it as the beginning of a new type of international super-company that would leverage its enormous capacity on both continents to increase profitability. Instead, it was a new type of money-losing international company. While Mercedes continued to make big profits because of its high-end market niche, Chrysler struggled through a downturn in its truck business and the enormous financial load of its 90,000 pensioners. Its pension liabilities had become so high that it was often described as a pension company with a car division.

By early 2007, it was clear to observers that the Chrysler/Daimler marriage had been a mistake. It was also obvious that Chrysler would be cheap for the buyer. Daimler made it clear that it wanted to unload its failed American sister in any way possible.

By March, the bidding had begun. A handful of private equity firms, including the behemoth Blackstone and Tracinda Corp., the personal investing arm of multibillionaire Kirk Kerkorian, put in what seemed to be low-ball bids of around $5 billion. Competitor General Motors made noise about possibly placing a bid as well.

Then Cerberus made its bid. On the surface, their bid appeared to be the highest: $7.8 billion. In fact, almost all of that money was not to be paid to Daimler, but to be reinvested into Chrysler. When the amount of cash that Chrysler had in its bank account (more than $4 billion) was taken into account, it turned out that Daimler was actually paying Cerberus to take Chrysler off its hands.

How could the Daimler executives have agreed to such a sweetheart deal for Cerberus? Because the other deals were linked to the approval of a new union contract with the UAW (United Auto Workers), which was scheduled to be negotiated later that fall. If a contract could not be agreed upon, the sale would be canceled and Chrysler would revert back to Daimler ownership.

All the bidders knew that if a strike were called, Chrysler could be mortally wounded. So the key to any deal revolved around the negotiations with the UAW. And Cerberus offered something that none of the other bidders offered: a good working relationship with the UAW.

As part of the preparatory work for their bid, Cerberus executives (including some ex-Chrysler executives they had hired to advise them) met with union leaders and established a good rapport with them. Although no agreements were put in place, they exchanged rough ideas of what a new UAW contract should look like. When it came time for Daimler to review the various bids, the UAW leaders let it be known that they would not oppose a Cerberus purchase. Daimler's primary motivation was to be rid of Chrysler and its deleterious effect on its financial statements. Cerberus did their homework and ensured that they completely understood the needs of Daimler before they started the negotiations. Because the company understood the real needs of Daimler, they offered the only deal that wasn't contingent on a union contract agreement and they therefore won the deal.

In September 2007, the newly-Cerberus-owned Chrysler sat down at the table with UAW negotiators and made a show of pressing hard for concessions. It turned out that the union did call a strike against Chrysler. But the strike lasted one day and a new three-year contract was signed, stunning many observers who were expecting a bitter struggle between the Wall Street financiers and the muscular union.

It's not yet clear whether Chrysler will successfully turn the corner on its troubles, but it is apparent that the new ownership and management have made enormous strides in changing the morale of the once mighty auto giant. Thousands of layoffs were made, but Cerberus hasn't gutted the company and sold its parts the way that some alarmists had predicted.

Cerberus incorporated a number of negotiating strategies here. It first correctly identified three stakeholders in the deal: itself, Daimler, and the UAW. Like Abraham and Moses, it then pursued an accommodative and nonconfrontational style with the union—very unlike its reputation. Like Moses, the Cerberus negotiators also made sure that they clearly understood the needs of Daimler, which was, above all else, to completely offload Chrysler. Thus, by bringing the union on board, Cerberus was able to negotiate an astoundingly advantageous price with Daimler for the actual purchase. And like the Jacob and Esau deal, it was win-win all around. Daimler achieved its goal of unloading Chrysler's enormous pension liabilities, and Cerberus got a great price on the automaker.

Using Questions and Creating Trust in Negotiations

There are unifying methods in the negotiating tactics of Abraham and Moses. Notice that they both began their negotiations with questions. Neither started off with an offer or a demand, and the questions they asked went to the heart of what God wanted. Abraham asked whether God was going to kill the righteous together with the wicked, thus hinting at a problem with justice. Moses asked God why He used unprecedented miracles to take the Israelites out of Egypt only to kill them later, indicating an issue with the perception of power. Abraham and Moses each asked respectful questions that required good answers.

This is an excellent strategy to use in negotiations. As Harry Mills writes in his book *The Streetsmart Negotiator* (Amacom, 2007), "Questions are among the most potent communication tools negotiators can use." Asking questions in negotiations has two main advantages. It makes a point without being confrontational and disrespectful, and it causes the person to think more deeply about the potential flaws of their position. If there is a good answer, it gives the other party the opportunity to better explain their situation. And finally, asking questions can circumvent the possibility of making incorrect assumptions regarding the other side's primary motivations.

In addition, both Abraham and Moses had built up an intense reservoir of trust with God, who knew that they were both faithful to Him and cared first and foremost about doing the right thing. They both had a proven track record of being loyal and trustworthy, creating a good relationship. If this had not been the case, there would not have been any negotiations at all.

Trust is vital in any negotiation, but especially where a large amount of money is at stake. If there is not a level of trust between the parties, there is no basis for a relationship. And certainly not for a deal. Trust must be built over time and it can either come through multiple personal dealings or by virtue of a good reputation. Whatever the case, trust-building must be a priority for anyone who wants to be successful at negotiating. As Harry Mills writes, "People with dishonest reputations don't get believed—even when they tell the truth. Professional negotiators therefore jealously protect their reputations for honesty."

> **INSIGHT FOR BUSINESS:** *If you ever need to get a point across that may not be taken well, it is better not to say it directly. There is another option: ask a pointed question that will make the other party realize on their own the point you want to make. Often by answering such a question, the other party will either clarify their position for you or they will realize the error of their position and move closer to yours.*

> **INSIGHT FOR LIFE:** *Realize that trust in interpersonal relationships takes time to build. However, without it there cannot be a rela-*

tionship. Take the time and effort to build trust, respect, and friendship with the people in your life.

Verifying the Terms of an Agreement

According to studies quoted by Robert E. Gunther, Stephen J. Hoch, and Howard C. Kunreuther in their book entitled *Wharton on Making Decisions* (Wiley, 2001), 28 percent of negotiators lie about common interest issues during negotiations. They also noted that 100 percent of negotiators either did not disclose problems or, if they were not directly asked about it, actually lied about them during the negotiations. This poses a dilemma about how to win in negotiations if the other side is not trustworthy. Biblical Jacob had exactly this dilemma. The story should already be familiar from the previous chapter, so we will just summarize it here.

Jacob had arrived at Laban's home and started working for him without pay for an entire month. After a month Laban offered to pay Jacob a salary for his work and the negotiations over compensation began. Note that before Jacob began negotiating with Laban he had proven his worth by working for a month and showing his talents and abilities. Now that Jacob had established himself as a good worker he was in a stronger negotiating position. But Jacob had fallen in love with Laban's younger daughter, Rachel, and wanted to marry her. Jacob agreed to work for Laban for seven years and in lieu of payment he asked Laban permission to marry the beautiful Rachel. Laban readily agreed, saying that it was worthwhile because he was in favor of giving his daughter to Jacob as a bride rather than to another man.

When the seven years were over, a wedding date was set, but Laban deceived Jacob. Instead of giving him the beautiful Rachel as a bride, Laban gave him the older and less pretty Leah to marry. When Jacob woke in the morning he realized that he had been conned and was understandably furious.

Now if we recall the earlier story where Jacob bought the birthright from Esau for a bowl of lentil soup, scripture tells us that he made Esau swear to the deal. Thus, he verified that the birthright had indeed been sold to him. Jacob, however, did not verify his deal with Laban, allowing Laban to justify his actions by saying that he was unable to give Rachel as a bride to Jacob because it was not their custom to give the younger daughter's hand in marriage before the older one. Had Jacob only verified the terms of his agreement with Laban, he would have been able to avoid the deceit he faced later on. This is instructive to us. Don't ever leave a negotiation without first verifying what you believe has been agreed upon. The best course of action is to draw up a memorandum or note of principal agreements that can then be shared between the two parties to ensure that both sides actually agreed upon the issues that were negotiated. The perceptions as to what had been agreed upon during negotiations between two parties can differ, and this makes it imperative that a document be drafted and that all parties sign off regarding the details of the negotiations.

Abraham, Jacob, and Moses all understood that hostile confrontation does not lead to successful negotiations. They also recognized that to negotiate effectively, it is important to understand the other side's position, including its needs, strengths, and weaknesses. There is great value in this. Only when we are able to really appreciate the other party's situation can there be a real understanding and ability to talk about the issues involved on a deeper level. Very often, when parties become entrenched in their own viewpoint during negotiations, they cannot see the viewpoint of the other side. This is why mediators are needed. Abraham and Moses knew that what God really wanted, and what they were aiming for was similar. All they had to do was to present it so that God was able to see how both of their interests matched.

This is true of most negotiations, even those that seem intractable. Often, common ground can be found. However, we often spend too much time preparing our own position and not enough trying to understand the other party's position. The result is that when the two sides come together we each take to our own corner and a middle ground is then difficult to find. In order to realize a successful conclusion to negotiations we must avoid confrontation and understand the needs of the other side.

INSIGHT FOR BUSINESS: *Negotiations can become incredibly complex. But very often, the simple things lead to breakdowns or poor deals. Remember to always verify what the other side's intentions are. Assumptions just aren't good enough—and can lead to disaster. Verify, verify, verify.*

INSIGHT FOR LIFE: *The more you allow yourself to be hurt by the behaviors of others and not realize that outer actions are a result of inner needs and feelings that we all share, the more likely resentment and even hate will come into play. Understand what really motivates others and if any relationship is to be preserved avoid jumping to conclusions at all cost.*

Meditation

Incorporating some of the ideas found in this chapter into your business negotiations may not be easy. Habits die hard, and changing negotiating tactics may be easier said than done. Meditative contemplation can help here. Before a major negotiation, take at least ten minutes to review what you know about the other side and what your negotiating strategy will be, based on what you have learned from this chapter and elsewhere. Once you are completely satisfied that your strategy has been laid out, begin your contemplation. Think about your negotiation strategy over again the first time in a general way. Then think it through again, this time delving deeper and spending more time thinking over each detail. Allow your strategy to remain in your mind going over it again and again. Remember, you are not trying to work out how you are going to negotiate—you have already done this. Now you are just ensuring that the techniques you have decided to use have really sunk in. As you contemplate on your negotiating strategy further and delve into the details again, you will feel that you have fully connected to your strategy. At this point, the negotiating techniques that you will use will be almost second nature and you will use them with ease and confidence.

CHAPTER 6

DEALING WITH FAILURE
Handling Failure to Ensure Future Success

Much wisdom comes through much grief.
—ECCLESIASTES 1:18

THAT ALL HUMANS FAIL AT SOME POINT IN THEIR LIVES IS AN IN-
escapable fact. According to the Torah, no human being is expected
to be perfect. Even Moses was deemed to have erred when he hit a
rock with his staff instead of speaking to it as God had asked him to
do. There is a message here: humans are by their very essence fallible.
Failing is just part of normal human life and there is no reason to be
alarmed when it happens. The challenge is the manner in which we
respond to failure: it can lead to more failures or to greater heights
of success.

Since failing is to be expected from time to time, there is no reason to get depressed when it happens. This is not to say that it's a
cause for celebration, but it certainly doesn't call for dejection or
self-flagellation either. The moment we realize that occasional failure is inevitable, and that it happens to even the most successful
people, its stigma is removed. We must also realize that failure in

business is often a result of our own individual and personal character flaws. When we stop making the same mistakes over and over again, real and sustained success follows. This chapter will suggest strategies to identify and overcome the flaws that cause us to fail in both business and life and in doing so will open up for us the doors of success.

Avoiding the Path to Massive Failure

Before we begin discussing ways to limit and respond to failure, it is important to explore how failure comes about. Monumental failures don't just happen; they are a culmination of many small mistakes. The late Lubavitcher Rebbe, Rabbi Menachem M. Schneerson (1902-1994), once asked the young Jonathan Sacks, who went on to become the British Chief Rabbi, what he was doing to help the Jewish students at Cambridge University, where he was studying. He began by answering, "In the circumstances I currently find myself . . ." The Lubavitcher Rebbe immediately interrupted him and said, "No one finds themselves in circumstances. We create our own circumstances." By realizing this fundamental truth, we can take control of the mistakes we make in our business and personal lives. We can avoid failure on a large scale by taking responsibility for our small mistakes and ensuring that they are not repeated.

Unfortunately, many of us do not spend much time being introspective and therefore continue making the same mistakes repeatedly. Due to embarrassment, we go into denial and find it difficult to admit, even to ourselves, that we err. And when massive failure hits, we find others to blame and then go on to make the same mistakes again. This is often why new businesses fail. Many entrepreneurs have multiple business failures until they begin to learn from their mistakes and figure out how to get it right.

Mistakes can and should be fixed right away. Benjamin Franklin is reputed to have said, "The definition of insanity is doing the same thing over and over and expecting different results." We all know that mistakes should not be repeated, but too few of us actually follow this advice. The reason is obvious: many people do not realize or are afraid to admit they are actually making mistakes. This creates failure in every aspect of our lives, in our careers, in our business lives, and in our personal relationships. Fortunately, the Torah offers a foolproof way to overcome and make the most out of failures—the lessons of which are as applicable to business as they are to religion.

> **INSIGHT FOR BUSINESS:** *Embarrassment about failure and mistakes has no place in business, where the bottom line always speaks the truth. If you do not own up to your mistakes and become cognizant of them, your entire enterprise will suffer as a result. Remember too that any business that is not on top of correcting mistakes made will soon have to deal with large-scale failure.*

> **INSIGHT FOR LIFE:** *Don't blame everything and everyone other than yourself for failure. By blaming others, you continually make the same mistakes and then wonder why your relationships never seem to work. It is important to look inside yourself when things are not going right. In most cases the problem lies within you.*

Fixing Our Failures

Living a religious life means trying to connect to God by doing what He wants and not doing the things that go against the Divine will. Every religious person will admit to failing from time to time and not living up to religious expectations. As King Solomon said (Ecclesiastes 7:20), "There is none righteous upon the earth who does only good and does not sin." Since all religious people sin, most religions provide a procedure people can follow to overcome their sins. In Judaism that process is called *t'shuva*.

Most often translated as "repentance," *t'shuva* literally means "returning." The act of repentance, according to the Torah, is more than just an oral declaration of wrongdoing. It is an elaborate process of defeating sin that includes articulation of that sin, cleansing ourselves of it, and promising to avoid repeating it. Upon proper completion of the process of *t'shuva*, we can return to walking in God's path.

To understand the concept of repentance it's useful to first explore the concept of sin. Take away the moral stain that tends to be attached to the act of sinning and what are you left with? A mistake. According to the Torah, sinning is more than just not following directions. It's also doing something that is counterproductive to one's own interests. A person doesn't follow God's laws just because they are written somewhere. One does so because they believe it is in their best interests as well. For a religious person, contravening God's laws is like making a personal mistake.

That is why the concept of repentance, which is usually only thought of in terms of moral or religious sin, is just as applicable to fixing business and other mistakes. If repentance is a way to fix an error, it can be applied to any type of blunder. It's important to emphasize here that we are not proposing that common business mistakes like procrastination or poor planning are somehow moral sins. But, just like moral or religious sins, they are fixable mistakes. And the Torah provides a protocol for how to fix mistakes and ensure that they are not repeated.

That protocol involves four steps. Let us look at each in some detail.

Recognize the mistake and take responsibility for it. The first is to recognize and take responsibility for the mistake and to realize the potential damage it does to our business or our lives. This takes significant depth of thought. A good example of a commonly repeated mistake is procrastination. For many, procrastination is a major stumbling block to real success. No matter how important a task may be, some people do not seem to ever leave themselves enough time to complete it properly. They simply procrastinate until they have run out of time, and the end product suffers considerably as a result. Because of this, they do not get repeat business and their reputation suffers. In addition, this causes increased stress and anxiety. If people are honest with themselves, they will realize that they have a problem. But fixing the problem is difficult. For this, you must acknowledge fully the damage procrastination is causing on every level. Through deep contemplation on the effects of this mistake, you will begin to see procrastination as the enemy—the thing that is standing between you and success—and this will motivate you to fight it properly the next time it appears. The same process can apply to many other problems, including anger, lack of focus, arrogance, and negativity.

Recognize the error in your thinking. Once you recognize the failure and how it negatively affects your life, you can advance to the second step: recognition of the error in your thinking that caused the mistake. We will use the mistake of arrogance to illustrate this step. Arrogance stems from the mistaken idea that you are of greater value than others. Since all humans are created in the Divine image, and as such are equal, this really means that the arrogant person thinks he or she is better than human. Such thinking comes dangerously close to idolatry. In this case, the idol is oneself. By carefully examining the thought process that leads to arrogance—or to any other character flaw that results in failure—you can identify where the logic is faulty and begin the process of fixing it.

Admit the mistake to yourself and others. The third step is for us to admit the mistake to ourselves and, just as importantly, to others. There is much wisdom behind this. A well-known life coach once said that the mere fact that his clients know that he will call and check up on them motivates them to execute their tasks efficiently. The idea is that as long as others in our lives are aware of our problems and mistakes, they will be able to motivate us to avoid making them. So if you admit your issues to those around you, you will find it more difficult to continue committing those mistakes. Returning to our example of procrastination, once we have admitted this problem to our colleagues, we will find it more difficult to engage in the habit. We are aware that everyone else knows the real reason we are late with the project. This will motivate us not to procrastinate. And the same will apply to the rest of our failings.

Promise yourself not to succumb again. The fourth step in this failure-busting protocol is to resolve not to follow that erroneous way of thinking. This can take the form of a simple verbal vow to yourself. Or, if that's too easy to break, it can be a personal written agreement—with yourself, your spouse, best friend, life coach, even with God—to change your thinking and behavior.

> **INSIGHT FOR BUSINESS:** *Recognizing that all businesses suffer setbacks and mistakes is not enough. You should find and use a proper strategy that will ensure that your business avoids repeated errors and setbacks. The use of contemplation is a powerful tool for overcoming destructive elements that affect the bottom line. Recognize the damage mistakes cause to your business's profitability and then see them as your enemy.*

> **INSIGHT FOR LIFE:** *Admit the problems you are having to others and once you decide to kick a negative habit let your friends and family know. This will make it much more difficult to return to that habit again.*

Daily Failures Lead to Daily Success

The Jewish mystics claim that one should go through this above-mentioned four-step process daily or, at the very least, semiweekly. They call this process *h'eshbon ha'nefesh,* or "audit of the soul," because it is a process of introspection that enables us to look within and identify our strengths and weaknesses. Each time you perform an audit of the soul you should contemplate the events of the last day or semiweekly period. Look for those areas where you are making mistakes. As soon as you identify the mistakes or failures, go through the four steps enumerated above. By doing this, each time you make a mistake or fail, you become more aware of the error and of the erroneous mindset that caused it. After you have completed the fourth step and have resolved never to make the same mistake again, you increase your power to resist the unconscious urge to repeat that error.

Too bad it's not quite this easy, one-two-three-four cured! Don't underestimate how hard it is to change your underlying nature. A person who has an anger problem, for instance, will probably never completely change. However, according to the great eleventh-century Jewish ethicist Bahya ibn Paquda, author of a book entitled *Duties of the Heart,* if an arrogant person continually acts with humility, although a tendency towards arrogance will remain, humility will become second nature. This is true as well with all other character flaws, and with the repeated failures we make in our work and our lives. If you can acclimatize yourself to resist the things that blight your life and business, then *not* doing those things will become your second nature. The challenge is to stop making mistakes and errors and then never repeat them again. For that to happen, the sages maintain, a daily or at least a semiweekly audit of the soul is necessary. We are not quite so demanding, but feel that to make lasting changes—and to ensure that little mistakes are not morphing into a catastrophic big one—you should perform your audit at least once a week.

In addition to helping to curtail behaviors and actions that lead to failure, an audit of the soul can reinforce positive and constructive mindsets, behaviors, and actions. While going through the audit of the soul and thinking about the events of the period being contemplated, you will notice that you did certain things right as well. Be aware of them too. To change your habits, you must be as attentive to your positive behaviors as you are cognizant of your mistakes and failings.

This protocol for fixing mistakes and failures applies to a business as much as it does to the individual. You should make an audit of the business in exactly the same way you would make an audit of your soul. In fact, since personal mistakes and character flaws will have an impact on business failures, an audit of your soul and an audit of your business are completely compatible and can be done simultaneously. While following this advice doesn't mean that you won't fail again, at least old errors will be repeated less often. Ultimately, fewer mistakes and more successes will make a positive impact on your business's bottom line.

MDC Holdings: Too Busy to Fail

In his early twenties, Larry Mizel, who was later to become a very successful real estate investor and philanthropist, was ready to get out of Oklahoma. Born in Tulsa in 1942, he had finished his undergraduate studies and one year of law school at the University of Oklahoma when he transferred to the University of Denver College of Law in 1965. Unlike many of his companions who sought legal careers, Larry's primary goal for law school was to unlock the secrets of his passion: business.

One night he made the fateful decision to stop by a café at the border of Denver's downtown area. It was a popular spot for young professionals. "Today you would call it networking," said Mizel. "But back then we didn't have such fancy names. We just called it hanging out." That autumn evening he made the acquaintance of real estate maven Burt Heimlich, who introduced him to his first real estate deal: an empty lot across the street near the corner of Mexico and Colorado Boulevard. Heimlich told Mizel that he was involved with a group of investors looking to build a ten story apartment building on the site. Mizel quickly evaluated the opportunity and decided to go for it.

Even though he was a full-time student at the time, he had $20,000 that he inherited from his grandfather. Upon meeting architect Roland Wilson, he invested $18,000 for a 10 percent interest in the project. The group successfully raised enough money to acquire the property and to secure the necessary construction financing.

For the next eighteen months, Mizel immersed himself in the project, allowing his studies to lay fallow. "I learned by doing on that project," Mizel said. "I probably did everything wrong, but I learned how to do it right the next time."

As the building rose, so did Mizel's passion for real estate development. "I woke up every morning and I couldn't wait to start working," he said. When asked if it was the creation of the building or the money that could be made which fed his passion, he shook his head. "It was the act of going forward. It was the act of turning nothing into something."

But before the project was complete, the partners realized that they had a problem: the checking account they had been using as their accounting system was nearly empty, while only 80 percent of the construction had been completed. Mizel would soon learn that almost every building project takes extra time and comes in over budget. But the investing group hadn't planned for this contingency.

It became abundantly clear that the project needed additional financing. Otherwise, as soon as the construction workers stopped receiving their paychecks, the lender would learn that that the project had stopped and would assume ownership. "We needed a way to keep the project going at a slow pace so we could get some time to find more financing." The problem was that nobody was willing to loan them money to complete a project that was already fully pledged as collateral for the initial loan.

Mizel and his partners could have surrendered the shell of a building to its creditor. But that would have gone against his primary rule in life: never, ever, ever, give up.

By that time, Mizel had already begun his second development project and was beginning to establish himself as a budding entrepreneur destined for success. Through hard work, focus, and dedication he emerged as somebody people were willing to take risks on for the sake of doing more business in the future. Mizel used his newfound credibility and his creativity to convince his vendors to finance part of their own work, and ultimately to obtain additional financing from other sources as well.

The building they completed in 1967, called the De Medici Apartments, still stands near the corner of Mexico and Colorado Boulevard, and Larry Mizel still owns his share. He is also the founder, chairman, and CEO of MDC Holdings, one of the nation's largest homebuilders, employing several thousand people and valued by the stock market in April 2008 at more than $2 billion, this even during one of the worst housing downturns in modern American history. MDC was founded in 1972 with an initial capitalization of $50,000.

Mizel has been through many scrapes in the rough and tumble business of real estate development since his first intoxicating experience with it in 1966. But he survived them and was strengthened by his challenges. Failure, he says, is an attitude, not an event. When asked how he responds to failure, he replied: "I don't know. I can't remember having experienced it—for me failure is never an option."

What in fact happened here was that Larry Mizel used his failure to make ends meet on the first project as a catalyst to start other projects. In addition, he took careful note of his first mistakes and, vowing never to make them again, was able to move on to a fabulously successful career in real estate. Although Mizel did not undertake the self-auditing protocol outlined above, he did make sure to identify small mistakes early on so that they were not repeated and thus never caused massive failure.

> **INSIGHT FOR BUSINESS:** *You should audit your soul as often as you audit your balance sheet. This will allow you to clearly know both the character flaws and the business mistakes that might cause the business to fail. The information gained from these audits can fend off large-scale failures. Do this as often as once a week.*

> **INSIGHT FOR LIFE:** *If there is a character trait causing you to fail, desist from that behavior. After a while, the absence of that negative trait will become second nature. The same applies if you want to incorporate a new positive behavior; faking it until you make it really works in that regard.*

Failure, Like Success, Is Deeply Personal

The self-auditing process practice is an effective way in which you can ensure that mistakes are stopped early on and never repeated. All successful businesspeople use mechanisms that provide similar results. However, an additional benefit and value of self-auditing is the positive way it helps us think about success and failure. The more we contemplate our own and our business's struggles and achievements, the better we are able to accurately assess the type of success we personally can achieve, in business and in our lives. Success and failure, therefore, becomes deeply personal, having nothing to do with what others are experiencing.

One of the great Jewish mystics, Rabbi Meshulam Zusha of Anipoli (1718–1800), said that in the next world the heavenly court would not ask him why he had not reached the level of achievements of biblical characters such as Abraham or Moses. Rather, he will be asked why he did not achieve what he, Rabbi Meshulam Zusha of Anipoli, was uniquely able to accomplish. Success is something that is expressly individual, and one person's success could be another's failure and vice versa. For example, it is impossible to compare the success of an ice cream store located by the beach in Miami to one located in a small town in Iowa. What is success for one would be failure for the other. The same is true with regard to individual talents and strengths. In other words, success is relative to an individual's circumstances, location, talents, and abilities. Comparing it to others that are not similar helps no one and is not a legitimate barometer of individual success.

This truth is lost on many people in the West, where success is symbolized by the amount of money you have amassed. If you drive an expensive car and have a large house, you are deemed by society to have succeeded. In reality, this may not be the case. Money and material possessions are not the only indication of having reached your own unique potential. Each person and business has different unique abilities and is able to make distinctive contributions to society and the economy. In Chapter 2 of this book you were guided to find your own unique abilities and authentic will. Here we are saying that no two people's abilities, and therefore their contributions, are the same. As the Talmud said (Brachot 58a), "Just like no two people have the same faces no two people think exactly alike." Each of us has a unique nuance and flavor that we are exclusively able to add to the world. If we are not able to tap into the abilities that are expressly our own, no matter how much money or status we might have, we have not fully succeeded. The same is true in business: each enterprise can have a uniquely individualized niche in which it can succeed.

The Talmud (Sanhedrin 37a) further says that each person is obligated to say, "The world was created for me." This does not mean that we should be egotists. It means that each of us has something unique to add to the world—something without which the world would be worse off. If you deny your own unique contribution, you are negating the very reason for your existence. Is there a failure bigger than that?

Through regular contemplation, you can learn what your contributions really are and what the best business niche, for you, can be. Then, successes and failures will begin to be evaluated not against others but rather by how you see your business, yourself, and your abilities. This knowledge is conducive to real success.

> **INSIGHT FOR BUSINESS:** *To find your business's niche, you must learn your own abilities and talents. Only through focused contemplation and personal audits can you be sure to find them.*

> **INSIGHT FOR LIFE:** *Don't compare your success and failure to those of others. Success is very personal, and what may be successful for another individual may be failure for you. Judge yourself on your unique set of talents and abilities.*

The Man Who Refused to See Failure

Several people who we interviewed for this book said that the word failure is not part of their vocabulary—no matter how bad things are, they never see a situation as being in a state of total collapse. The best example of a person with this attitude is David Slager, a partner in the hedge fund Atticus Capital. "The word failure is too terminal," Slager said. "Situations are rarely all over. There is normally a chance to redeem oneself."

David Slager said that this approach to setbacks was inspired by a Talmudic figure known as Nachum Ish Gam Zu, a name which literally translates as "Nachum the Man of Also This." The Talmud (Ta'anit 21a) explains that he got the name because no matter how bad the situation was, he had a tendency to always say *gam zu letova,* meaning "This, too, is for the good." In other words, for Nachum Ish Gam Zu there was no such thing as a terrible outcome—from his perspective, everything was for the good. And if that fact was not apparent in the moment, time would show that it was so.

Mirroring this approach, David Slager differentiates between personal misjudgments and the overall outcome. Admitting that no one is perfect and mistakes are inevitably made, Slager says, "I may have made a misjudgment, but what happens in the end is for the good—*gam zu letovah*—whichever way the stock market treats me is for the good." Illustrating this point, he says "I very rarely give up on an investment. I am known in the office for being the one who very rarely changes his mind or very rarely gives up on something. So when an investment seems to fail, I normally view it as an opportunity to buy more, more cheaply."

"There are two ways of looking at a negative situation," David Slager explains. "When a stock I am investing in goes down, for example, I could look at it and say that it was a costly lesson but I learned from it. But the more positive way of thinking is that it is an opportunity to buy more of it. Often when an investment goes down it is an opportunity for the good."

This concept is vital to ensuring that mistakes will not remain permanent and will eventually lead to success. For some, failure leads to a form of self-identification. These people are unable to see the silver lining in things—when their stocks are down, they are down personally as well. But for those who are able to see the silver lining within everything, for those who realize that there are forces beyond their own control, real personal failure does not exist. Such people are always able to see the upside of the cards the universe has dealt them. While they may admit to have made a misjudgment or a mistake, it never ends in total failure. Beneath each failure lies something positive—what to others may be perceived as failure is for them a potential for future success.

This approach changes the way one deals with challenging situations. The person who only sees failure will bail out of an investment when it starts to plummet, or will give up on a business that begins to falter. Not people with David Slager's approach, though. They have the ability to stay with an investment even as it gets really tough and others are pulling out. This is the key to success, says Slager, "The winners in this business are those who are not shaken easily," or, to quote the great inventor Thomas Edison, "Many of life's failures are men who did not realize how close they were to success when they gave up."

> **INSIGHT FOR BUSINESS:** *While most businesses make mistakes, you should never label your enterprise a failure. When your business seems to be failing, look for the silver lining to it—all successful businesses have been at that stage, yet have overcome. All you need to do is see beyond the here and now and have faith in a brighter future.*

> **INSIGHT FOR LIFE:** *Remember that real personal failure is a state of mind rather than a state of being. We all make mistakes but you are only a failure if you allow yourself to be one.*

Shames-Makovsky Realty Corporation: The End of the Line Is Just the Start of the Journey

After fifteen years in the Denver real estate business, Evan Makovsky thought he had seen everything. But the economic downturn of the mid-1980s was like nothing he had ever experienced. He had built his brokerage business, then Shames & Makovsky Realty, into a success through the proven method of wearing out the pavement. As a young realtor, he built a clientele of small businesspeople who appreciated his dedication and skill when the bigger Denver brokerages wouldn't give them the time of day.

Over time, the firm had grown to a million-dollar business with sixteen employees and a reputation for exceeding the expectations of clients. But the Denver real estate market went from bad to worse in the 1980s. As the energy crisis abated and oil prices dropped, money flowed out of the state of Colorado and left office buildings empty and houses for sale. At the same time, a credit crunch made local banks less willing to make business loans. As each month went by in 1986 and 1987, Makovsky saw his revenues declining. He borrowed money personally in order to continue meeting his payroll, but he had reached his own credit limit. By mid-1987, he had come to the end of the road. He was staring into the abyss of bankruptcy. The real estate market seemed to have dealt his business a devastating if not fatal blow. But for Evan Makovsky, setbacks, even very large and threatening ones, always had a silver lining.

It was all the more frustrating to him because he knew that many of his clients wanted to buy or lease properties and had nearly enough money to do so, but just couldn't get enough credit from their bankers; at the time banks were only willing to lend 50 percent of the value on commercial buildings. That's when Makovsky had his epiphany. He would add a new element to his company. In addition to being a commercial real estate brokerage, he would also become a real estate lender specializing in bridging loans. If a client could get 50 percent of the needed capital from a bank, he would lend them the other 25 percent, leaving the buyer to come up with only a 25 percent deposit.

All he needed was capital. And he got it from his old clients, the mom-and-pop store owners and small businesspeople with whom he had built up a relationship over the previous fifteen years. As Shames-

Makovsky had grown, so too had these businesses. And they now wanted a safe place to invest their money. Makovsky wanted to pool the funds of his trusted long-time clients and use that money to underwrite low-risk loans for other clients.

So one day in the summer of 1987 he called a general meeting of all his staff in the company conference room. When Makovsky entered the room, all his employees and brokers were there. Some of them were crying, assuming that he was about to announce the end of the company. "They all knew how bad things were, so they expected that we were all just going to leave the office right then and there and leave the key in the door," he recalled.

Instead, Makovsky delivered a passionate pep talk, during which he outlined his new plan to transform Shames-Makovsky Realty from a simple broker into a brokerage/lender hybrid. The staff took the idea and ran with it. Within months, the company had turned the corner and was once again growing in size. When he determined that he would have to make new hires to keep up with the new business, Evan Makovsky realized that the crisis was over.

In fact, he and his firm were about to embark on a prolonged boom. They soon had a large portfolio of properties throughout Denver and he made the decision to transform the firm from a simple commercial real estate brokerage to a brokerage with a mortgage company attached to it.

Once Evan Makovsky's investors began to get back the money they had invested with Evan, they said to him, "We don't just want a return *of* our investment—we want a return *on* our investments." This took Shames-Makovsky into a new direction. Instead of brokering a sale between a buyer and a seller they began to raise capital to invest in commercial real estate themselves. If a buyer wanted to sell a property and Makovsky was able to find a tenant for the property, he would find investors and buy the property and then allow the tenant to rent it from him; this way he was able to make impressive returns for his investors. So now Shames-Makovsky Realty was also a real estate investment and property management company. As such profitable investment real estate became scarcer, Shames-Makovsky Realty moved into developing properties. Makovsky would build properties that he knew he could lease out in order to make more money for his investors and for his company. Within a few years of facing total failure and bankruptcy, Shames-Makovsky Realty has bounced back stronger, bigger and better than before. Now, instead of being a commercial real estate brokerage, the firm encompasses a commercial real estate development company, a property management company, a real estate investment company, and a mortgage company. If not for the potential failure Evan Makovsky and his company faced in 1987, he would never have moved in the direction he did and would have lost out on the opportunities that ensued.

Clearly, the difference between those who fail and those who ultimately succeed is their approach to failure. To people like Evan Makovsky and David Slager, failure is never an option, and no matter how bleak the outlook, there is always a silver lining. The continuation of the story of the Israelites and the golden calf (told in Chapter 5) further illustrates how a successful person must view failure.

Seeing Failure as Freedom: The Second Set of Tablets

As Moses came down the mountain and saw the Israelites performing pagan rituals around the golden calf, he dropped and broke the two tablets that he had received from God on top of Mount Sinai and upon which the Ten Commandments had been inscribed (Exodus 32:19). Later (Exodus 34:28), Moses ascended the mountain again to receive a second set of tablets from God with the same words inscribed upon them.

According to the mystics, the first set of tablets, inscribed and carved by the perfect Divine hand (figuratively speaking), represent the erroneous idea that we can be perfect without blemishes. Thus, when the handiwork of the Creator came down to earth among imperfect humans, that ideal vision came face to face with the stark reality of the frailty and fallibility of the created. When something that requires perfection is confronted with deficiency and failings, it cannot function and quickly breaks down. This is what happened to the first set of tablets: they could not handle the inherent imperfections of the Israelites and thus ended up broken.

The second set of Tablets that Moses received, tradition says, was of a different nature. They were dictated by God but carved by Moses, a human being. Thus, a human, inherently fallible, was a part of their makeup. According to the mystics, God designed it this way. He wanted there to be a second set of tablets—He wanted the perfect ideal to be pierced by failure. The reason for this, say the mystics, is because failure allows the individual to reach ever greater heights of success. As King Solomon said (Ecclesiastes 1:18), "Much wisdom comes through much grief." Thus, as a result of the creation of the second Tablets, tradition has it that God revealed additional details of His Divine wisdom, now known as the oral law, to Moses and through him to the Israelites. So, as a result of the failure of faith that was the sin of the golden calf, greater success was realized. This point was not lost on Torah thought. Through the second set of Tablets, it became clear that any perceived failure, if handled properly, has the potential for eventual success. And after the shattering of any perfect vision there is always the potential for a second chance that will deliver results that are superior to what the first perfect idea, vision, or project was able to yield.

An enterprise that is not working properly limits entrepreneurs, not allowing them to reach their full potential. When an enterprise fails totally and irrevocably, however, they are forced to find a solution from a different direction, leaving them, unencumbered by failure, to follow their ultimate dreams and desires. The failing project no longer consumes their energy and the opportunities are endless. If perfection were always expected, then people would feel obligated to avoid failure at all costs which would therefore limit the desire to try risky enterprises, businesses, and investments. If seen in the way discussed above, failure is really just a stepping stone to another success. As the saying goes, "The path to success is paved with failures." But when shown in this light it is no longer really a failure, rather just another step towards success.

In addition, when viewed through this prism, failure can be incredibly instructive. Often, when we fail, it is because we are not quite suited to run that particular enterprise or project. Thus, failure can be seen as a signpost on the path to success that shows us the direction we must take and gently—or not so gently—guides us off a path we are not meant to tread. In this sense, failure does not really exist. Rather, it is a correctional device that leads us to the path of success. If we are afraid of failure however, we may never reach success. This is what successful people mean when they say that failure is never an option.

Many people have made this point. Playwright George Bernard Shaw said, "A life spent making mistakes is not only more honorable but more useful than a life spent doing nothing." Theodore Roosevelt said, "He who makes no mistakes makes no progress." Thomas Edison said, "I am not discouraged, because every wrong attempt discarded is another step forward," and "I have not failed. I've just found ten thousand ways that won't work."

Stanley Prusiner: Finding Success in Failure

It used to be that science was a separate domain from business, filled with white-coated idealists who pursued knowledge for the sake of knowledge and left making money to those who wore pin-striped suits. Those days are long gone. Science has become a business that involves multimillion-dollar deals, complex organizational structures, and strategic alliances. That's not to mention the bitter competition for tenured appointments and grants.

The business of science is the most extreme example of an enterprise that needs a positive attitude towards failure to really succeed. When an experiment goes as expected, something that was predicted is confirmed. When the results go counter to expectations—in other words, when they fail—something new is often discovered. Stanley Prusiner's story offers a wonderful example of this.

Prusiner was a medical researcher working at the University of California at San Francisco, one of the world's most prestigious research institutions. Prusiner had become fascinated by the case of a patient who had died at the University hospital from an unidentified virus that had been called by his colleagues a "slow virus." Its presence appeared in a female middle-aged patient and had taken months before it finally killed her. Upon autopsy, the doctors found her brain to be filled with hard, plaque-like particles located in the midst of holes in the tissue. This unknown virus had literally eaten away her brain.

Prusiner dedicated his research enterprise to this woman's disease, but because this virus was so rare, he began studying a similar disease, scrapie, which appears only in sheep. It acts in sheep as this virus does in humans—striking the animals in their prime and leaving behind calcified granules in the brain cavity after death. Prusiner found that he could take scrapie samples and use them to infect lab mice—shortening the time it took to study the disease's progress even more.

After collecting numerous samples from his scrapie-afflicted mice, Prusiner searched for the genetic code of the virus that caused the disease. To do that, he washed the samples numerous times, using various chemicals to take everything out of the test tube except the nucleic acids—the genetic material around which genes are built. All Prusiner had to do was to remove the amino acids—the building blocks of proteins—and the nucleic acids would be left behind. But no matter how many times he ran the experiment, no nucleic acids were left in the test tube.

By that time, Prusiner had spent years trying to discover the organism that causes scrapie, which would then open the door to identifying the virus that causes "slow virus." But he had little to show for his work and the university and his financial backers were threatening to terminate his funding. Such a move would have effectively ended his career. Produce something soon, they told him, or you'll have to find a new line of work. To a scientist, research grants are as valuable as life's blood. Without them, all activity in the laboratory stops and soon the job itself is at risk. At this point in his life, Prusiner was facing a serious cash flow problem.

Amid these pressures, Prusiner had an idea. His failure to find nucleic acids—and hence a possible viral cause—led him to consider the impossible. What if the lack of nucleic acids in his samples was due to the disease being caused by a protein, not a virus? Such a hypothesis flew in the face of several basic rules of biology. Proteins, as we learned in Biology 101, are inert. They don't replicate. They don't grow. They don't encode information that can be passed on to future generations. That's what viruses, bacteria, and human beings do. And they all use nucleic acids to encode their genetic blueprints.

But Prusiner was now proposing a model that ran counter to those basic assumptions of science. He postulated that the cause of scrapie was a protein that folded itself wrongly. The misfolded protein then somehow caused other, nearby proteins to misfold into harmful structures. As they built up, they formed the calcified granules that become the hallmark of scrapie, "slow virus," and even Alzheimer's disease. Prusiner was suggesting that all those diseases were caused by a non-living molecule that reproduced itself. He even coined a term for these toxic proteins, calling them "prions."

In the immediate aftermath of his landmark paper's publication in 1982, Prusiner was almost universally derided. Colleagues in his field made derogatory comments about him to the press, accusing him of fraudulent science. The only reason they couldn't prove him wrong, they said, was because they hadn't found the virus behind the diseases yet. When they did find it, they would reveal Stanley Prusiner to be a fool. He was shouted down at scientific conferences and shunned by many leading scientists.

But Prusiner's rivals never could find the virus that caused scrapie, despite repeated attempts. And other scientists kept finding data to back up Prusiner's theory. Nearly a decade after he first proposed it, most scientists in the field had come to accept the concept that misfolded proteins cause this malevolent class of diseases.

Prusiner, meanwhile, had captured the attention of significant financial backers and funding agencies and was able to obtain several multi-million-dollar grants. He had gone from nearly losing his job to reaching the pinnacle of success as a scientist. He went on to find the same evidence for prions in the other "slow virus" illnesses, including Creutzfeldt-Jacob disease, Kuru, and Alzheimer's disease, as well as in mad cow disease (officially, bovine spongiform encephalopathy), which is unfortunately transmissible to humans.

In 1997, Prusiner got his ultimate vindication: a Nobel Prize in medicine. The Nobel committee referred to his revolutionary theory as only one reason for the awarding of the prize to him. The prize was also awarded to him for his dogged determination to always see the silver lining inherent in what others might have assumed to be a failure. Without perceived failure, Stanley Prusiner would have never found success. In this sense, Prusiner never failed at all.

INSIGHT FOR BUSINESS: *Take the word "failure" out of your vocabulary. Any setback in business should be seen as a prelude to greater success. A setback can free you from enterprises and in-*

vestments that have not worked and will not work and allow you to seek better ways to succeed. Failure should be seen as a signpost along the road to success.

INSIGHT FOR LIFE: *If you see yourself as being perfect, you will eventually come face to face with the stark reality of imperfection. Recognize that mistakes and setbacks are a part of life, but that they can have positive results if you respond to them in the correct manner.*

Meditation

Spend time meditating on the way you spent your day. Make a mental note of all the things that went well and then make a note of all the mistakes made and the perceived failures that occurred. See whether you can detect a trend in the mistakes that you are making. Next, determine what mindset, what flawed thought process, caused you to make the mistakes. Ask yourself whether this mindset causes you to make other mistakes as well. Once you have done this, recognize that your flawed mindset and the mistakes that result are standing between you and greater success. Meditate on this point. Allow yourself to become upset for allowing the problematic issues to fester without dealing with and eliminating them. Recognize that this erroneous way of thinking is your real enemy. Contemplate on this deeply, allowing it to really sink in. Make a resolution to change your way of thinking so that the mistake and failure will be eliminated. Revisit this meditation at least once a week. The more you do so, the more mistakes you will eliminate. While you will never be able to eliminate mistakes completely, the more you do, the closer you will get to sustained success.

CHAPTER 7

SPIRITUAL ENTREPRENEURSHIP

Finding the Holy in Your Work

The choicest first fruit of your land you shall bring to the House of the Lord, your God.

—EXODUS 23:19

MANY OF US HAVE MET WEALTHY, FINANCIALLY SUCCESSFUL PEOPLE who are deeply unhappy. And, though we probably should not be, we are often surprised. Western culture teaches us that making money and achieving financial independence are the gateway to happiness. Conventional wisdom has it that the more money a person makes, the more contented they become. Capitalism offers the promise of ever-rising standards of living and material rewards for those who participate fully and intelligently in the game of business.

The problem is that as the game rolls on, the participants rarely find real happiness and contentment amid the lush goods and services they enjoy. They often feel that what they have is not enough and is not bringing the happiness they seek. They therefore pursue even more of it. When they feel depressed and empty inside, they just go to the mall to buy something. Sometimes it works for a while. The problem is that they have only bought themselves a temporary reprieve from a spiritual pain—a painkiller that deals with the symptoms of the depression rather than with the main cause of it. Within a short time, the feeling of emptiness returns.

As discussed in Chapter 2, real contentment and happiness comes only from following our inner will and authentic passion. And, in fact, many people today are seeking an alternative to the seemingly self-indulgent pursuit of making money. Some people enter the non-profit sector or become religious workers. And some are turning to a new fad in the business world called social entrepreneurship. This chapter will examine three models of entrepreneurship and will offer an alternative vision for how we can turn the moneymaking process into a deeply fulfilling pursuit and, as a byproduct, make even more money.

First however, it is important to point out that the Torah views the making of money as a potentially good thing. As we shall see, profiting can even be considered an act of piety under certain conditions. Being rich is seen as a sign of success in the Torah. A candidate for the position of high priest in the ancient Temple in Jerusalem, for example, needed to be wealthy to qualify for the job. The reason for this is because financially successful people are often successful in other areas as well, and would therefore be good administrators and wise decision makers. In addition, prosperity was seen as an indication of God's trust in the individual, on whom He had bestowed the blessings of wealth. We argue in this chapter that spiritual success and financial accomplishments are not only compatible, they can actually join in complete synthesis. We will show you, the entrepreneur, how you can turn the purely material pursuit of wealth into an act of piety.

Three Models of Entrepreneurship

There are at least three models of entrepreneurship: classic entrepreneurship, social entrepreneurship, and spiritual entrepreneurship. Whereas some people do business in a way that incorporates all of the three models, in the interests of clarity and to better explain them the three models are discussed individually.

Traditional western culture offers classic entrepreneurship as the way to do business. In recent years, postmodernism has nominated a new model—social entrepreneurship—to supersede the status quo. The Torah, on the other hand, has always offered the concept of spiritual entrepreneurship as a way to build a business and get closer to God simultaneously. Such a model results in a more fulfilling work life and career. It is a radically different approach to doing business that emphasizes making money as its main goal, but not for the sake of wealth alone. The entire moneymaking process can be sanctified so that it becomes a holy and noble pursuit. For this to happen, however, you need to completely change your focus. To understand this concept better, let's first explore the classic model of entrepreneurship.

Classic Entrepreneurship

Classic entrepreneurship is the way business has been done for the last few centuries (since the dawn of modern capitalism). Risks are taken by the entrepreneur in order to promulgate a new business idea and make it work. Its main goal is to create a new product or entity that will make money. Clearly, at the outset, classic entrepreneurship focuses on one aim: making as much money as possible.

Classic entrepreneurs take risks with their own capital and financial future because they want to become rich. There is no hidden agenda. The bottom line is the only factor. For classic entrepreneurs, business is business. While entrepreneurs enjoy creating new enterprises, the bottom line is strictly about profitability and wealth creation. Classic entrepreneurs don't go into business thinking about all of the benevolent things they might be able to do with the money. Helping others or making the world a better place is not on the agenda. Needless to say, this is the most self-gratifying form of entrepreneurship and is as far away from spirituality as one can imagine.

DONALD TRUMP: THE PROTOTYPE CLASSIC ENTREPRENEUR

Donald Trump is famous for his high-profile real estate investments as well as for his television show *The Apprentice*. He once said, "I wasn't satisfied just to earn a good living. I was looking to make a statement." But what kind of statement is he making? His entire business career has been motivated by making ever bigger deals and therefore making more money. While he says that the money is not the main motivation for him, he admits that it is the way he keeps score. Clearly, for a successful classic entrepreneur such as Donald Trump, business has one main goal and that is making successful deals that increase either the bottom line or his own sense of self importance. Illustrating this, Trump once said, "The point is that you can't be too greedy." A clear-cut statement.

The problem with the classic model of entrepreneurship is that after reaching the goal of making a lot of money, there is nothing else—emptiness often abounds. To quote Trump again: "I don't make deals for the money. I've got enough, much more than I'll ever need. I do it to do it." In other words, like many other classic entrepreneurs who have already made it and no longer need to work to survive, Mr. Trump goes to work each day in order to work—life has no meaning beyond the deal itself. Business is done for the sake of business, nothing else. No ulterior or higher motive comes into play. It's clearly not a recipe for a fulfilling and complete life.

INSIGHT FOR BUSINESS: *Classic entrepreneurship values business as being solely a method of making money. It requires a zero sum viewpoint, where business and spirituality can never mingle.*

INSIGHT FOR LIFE: *If you think that spirituality and your nine-to-five life can never mix together, open your mind to other possibilities. According to the Torah, the physical world, as painful, imperfect, and sullied as it is, is a highly spiritual plane of existence. Our task as spiritual beings is to reveal the spirituality inherent in the physical world, not to seek it elsewhere.*

Social Entrepreneurship

The concept of social entrepreneurship is relatively new, and while it is more advanced—at least morally speaking—than classic entrepreneurship, the problem is that it has not yet proven to be as much of a moneymaker. While many corporations have declared social goals and engage in charitable actions as part of their corporate mission, social entrepreneurship involves starting a company with the aim of making the world a better place in some way and trying to make money along the way.

MUHAMMAD YUNIS: THE PROTOTYPE SOCIAL ENTREPRENEUR

Amid the aftermath of the catastrophic floods of 1974 in Bangladesh, a young American-trained economist named Muhammad Yunis visited a ruined village to see how he could help. A group of families approached him and refused his offers of charity. Give us a small loan, they told him, and we will use it to start a business using our crafts. Once they started making money, they told Yunis, they could repay the loan as well as rebuild their homes and lives.

Yunis lent the families twenty-seven dollars. They repaid the loan quickly and they rebuilt their village while the surrounding villages remained stagnant. The experience gave Yunis an idea. We all know, he thought, that poor people don't have enough food, health care, and access to education. But maybe the thing that is really holding them back is the fact that they have no ability to borrow money. So he created a lending institution called Grameen Bank (which means "Bank of the Villages" in the Bangla language) whose sole purpose was to lend small amounts of money to the rural poor that could be used start new small businesses. Thus was born a new financial term: "microcredit."

Along the way, something else was born: a bank whose primary purpose is to help borrowers, not to make profits. Nonetheless, while Grameen Bank accepts donations from the West through its non-profit arm, the institution itself is structured as a for-profit endeavor.

The Grameen Bank has done tremendous good work in the last three decades. It has loaned out billions of dollars to more than six million Bangladeshis. It has empowered villagers, mostly women, to create new lives for themselves above and beyond what was possible prior to its establishment. And it has inspired hundreds of similar institutions throughout the world, in countries rich and poor, all of which are attempting to do some form of poverty alleviation through microcredit loans.

Indeed, the Grameen Bank deserves all the laurels it can get—including the Nobel peace prize, which its founder, Muhammad Yunis, received in 2006. But the founding of Grameen gave birth to an idea that hasn't been as successful at solving social problems: social entrepreneurship. Others throughout the world saw a for-profit bank that was doing so much good in the world and proclaimed that a new age had dawned for capitalism. Making money could be combined with making the world a better place. The idea really took root after the Internet boom, as hundreds of newly minted millionaires in their twenties looked for new ways to find meaning in their lives. They had succeeded in the fast-paced business world of Silicon

Valley, but their sudden influx of money had left them feeling hollow inside. Why not mix their passion for business with a beneficial social goal? Why not fix the world and make yourself even richer at the same time?

The Problem with Social Entrepreneurship

As most of those "businesses" have discovered in the years since their founding, there's a good answer to that question: when we try to fix the world and make money, we too often end up doing neither very well. Grameen Bank is a good example. As of the end of 2005, it had loaned out $5.72 billion since its inception. But it had only been paid back $5.05 billion. In other words, Grameen Bank is a money-losing company.

In that particular case, it didn't matter. Its for-profit status was merely an accounting peculiarity. Nobody expected Grameen Bank to make a profit. And, unlike other charities that give away money, Grameen has lost only about $680 million in its thirty years of operation. But it can hardly be called a successful business.

Other attempts at social entrepreneurship have been even less successful. Several businesses made the mistake of openly claiming that they were going to turn a profit and act as a charity at the same time. One example is the efforts of Pierre Omidyar, one of the founders of eBay, whose stake in that company is said to be worth more than $8 billion. Unlike other Internet tycoons who went on to build new companies, Omidyar set out to establish a venture capital fund for socially entrepreneurial startups. He wanted to be the venture capitalist for the next generation of for-profit charities. He also developed a special Website, called www.omidyar.net, to create a community of people who would brainstorm ideas for such enterprises.

To date, Omidyar.net has invested more than $30 million in for-profit charities. However, none have yet gained the prominence of

Grameen Bank. In July of 2007, he closed down the community website he had developed after it failed in its mission of attracting people and ideas.

We cannot criticize Pierre Omidyar for his goodwill, nor do we wish to. He is, after all, donating a lot of money to worthy causes. But we do disagree with his philosophy that a for-profit company is the best way to attain charitable goals. This is what he told a *New York Times* reporter in 2006: "If you look at the Grameen Bank, that is a business; you can't call it anything else . . . Its revenues are greater than its expenses, and it is tremendously effective in pulling people out of poverty. It is proof that you can have it both ways."

But the Grameen Bank isn't proof that you can have it both ways. The only way an accountant could claim that it makes a profit is if charitable donations to it are counted as revenue. Otherwise, it is a money-losing business.

Others have voiced a more severe criticism of social entrepreneurship beyond the philosophical arguments over whether it is the best way to structure a charity. Mark Rosenmann, a professor of philanthropy and finance at the Union Institute and University in Cincinnati, questioned the motivations of for-profit charities in the same *New York Times* article, saying, "Though I have no problem with philanthropy and socially responsible business being joined, I do have one with a for-profit enterprise being called philanthropy."

INSIGHT FOR BUSINESS: *The classic entrepreneur has at least part of it right. Business must focus on the goal of having a healthy income statement. You should not be tempted to make your business into some sort of social healing enterprise—while it might make a small difference for some people, or even a large difference for a few people, the bottom line will probably suffer.*

INSIGHT FOR LIFE: *Don't mix your goals. Stay individually focused on each thing you want to achieve. If you are on vacation with your family, for example, focus on that—if you try and mix your goals you will end up achieving poorly on all counts.*

Spiritual Entrepreneurship

While the goals and energy of social entrepreneurs are laudable, social entrepreneurship has yet to prove that it's the proper vehicle for attaining social goals and that it is a medium that can really make money. Non-profit organizations are far more successful and effective at changing the world. Business should not be confused with charity. At the same time, making money need not be entirely separated from living a spiritual life—it can and should be compatible. We call the concept of synthesizing spirituality and making money "spiritual entrepreneurship."

Spiritual entrepreneurship is very different from social entrepreneurship, both in form and in function. Whereas the focus of the latter is to make money out of doing good things for society, the former's focus is making money out of any profitable enterprise that is legal and ethical. Whereas social entrepreneurs attempt to transform business into a vehicle for social change, spiritual entrepreneurs use the money made from business to effect change. While social entrepreneurs only pursue business opportunities that will drive social change, spiritual entrepreneurs never pass up a legal and ethical opportunity to make money. Spiritual entrepreneurs see business as a means to an end rather than an end in itself. Besides their desire to make money, their agenda is also to use the money to improve the world in the manner that is congruent with what they perceive as God's purpose for the universe.

There is another important difference between spiritual entrepreneurs and classic entrepreneurs. Many businesspeople give money to charity and some religious people even tithe their income (which means giving 10 percent—or more than that if you desire—of your income to charity). Their main goal, however, is making money, not giving it away to charity. They are in business primarily to increase their standard of living and personal wealth. The spiritual entrepreneur, conversely, sees his or her entire moneymaking enterprise through the prism of the higher cause that the money could ultimately serve. This does not mean that spiritual entrepreneurs will not have real passion for the business that they are involved in—to be sure they will. But for them there is much more to making money than simply status or wealth creation. Spiritual entrepreneurs see money as a tool with which they can achieve things for the world. They see wealth as a God-given blessing of which they are the guardians. They feel a responsibility to use their money for higher purposes that go beyond selfish desires for more material possessions.

The following incident illustrates this difference. There was a recent debate on the radio during which one presenter was arguing against giving money to charity. He said, "I have worked hard for my money and I want to keep it for myself. I work hard to be able to have a nice car, a beautiful home, and a holiday, so why should I give my money to poor people? If they want more money then they should work hard like I did!" This might seem to be a very reasonable position to take. Indeed, why should people give away their hard-earned money to others? As long as they pay their taxes, shouldn't they be able to enjoy the rest of their money? Why should they deprive themselves of some of life's luxuries just because others have less than they do? While this argument makes sense to some who see the outer veneer of the universe as the sum total of all that exists, to those who are able to fathom the deeper reality of existence this argument is untenable.

To illustrate this, let us examine what the Torah says about charity and giving to others. The Torah elucidates why charity and tithing brings wealth. The verse states (Numbers 5:9): "And every portion from any of the holies that the children of Israel bring to the priest shall be his." According to tradition, the word "holies" refers to the first fruits of the fields, about which it is written (Exodus 23:19): "The choicest first fruit of your land you shall bring to the House of the Lord, your God." The verse in the book of Numbers, according to the commentators, adds to this that once the first fruits are brought to the House of the Lord they must be given to the priest.

The fact that the Torah separates these two details of bringing the first fruit to the House of the Lord, written in the book of Exodus, and giving the first fruit to the priest, written in the book of Numbers, adds meaning. Since growing fruit takes a tremendous amount of effort—you must plow, sow, nurture, harvest, etc.—you may think: after all this hard work at least let me enjoy the first fruit. Why should the priest get it? It was I who worked hard, not him.

But the Torah tells us explicitly in the book of Exodus that before the owner may eat from the fruit, "The choicest first fruit of your land you shall bring to the House of the Lord, your God." We need to realize that the fruit we grow does not really belong to us at all, but to God. It is He who provided the correct weather and environment for the fruit to grow. Without God there would be no fruit. Once the farmer recognizes this fact, it becomes less difficult for him to part with the first fruits and give them to the priest.

This is the way the Torah looks at all forms of livelihood. The giving of the first fruit to the priest is analogous to the modern day act of giving money to charity. The Torah tells us that we must tithe our income and give at least 10 percent of it to charity. Like a good year of farming, wealth is a blessing from Above and we must acknowledge it as such. God entrusts us with money and only asks that they part with at least 10 percent and give it to the charity of our choice.

The other 90 percent can be spent in any way we wish. After internalizing this fact, it becomes much easier to give money to charity.

In fact, it becomes absurd not to give to charity. Imagine that your biggest client asks you to give 10 percent of your fee to a charity. Would you say no? If you did you would lose the client: he or she would find someone else who would agree to that condition. Similarly, we get the blessings of abundance from the Divine energy. The condition, though, is that we donate at least 10 percent of it to charity.

In addition, the Divine promises us that the givers will not lose from tithing. On the contrary, they will only gain. In the merit of giving at least 10 percent of our income to charity we will receive real wealth. As the Torah says in Numbers (quoted above), "What a man gives to the priest shall be his." The Talmud (Brachot 63a) explains this verse to mean that in the merit of giving charity our income will increase greatly.

So wealth, according to the Torah, is not something that we automatically receive just because we work hard for it. To be sure, hard work is needed but real financial success does not come without a blessing from God. Just think of all the people you know who have sought wealth and have, for one reason or another, been unable to attain it. Now think about those who were successful because they happened to be in the right place at the right time. Without the blessing of being in the right place at the right time, real success eludes the seeker. It is important to understand that without that Divine energy, real and sustained financial success is impossible. This seems like a good deal. The Divine energy helps us to get the wealth and all it asks for is a 10 percent commission. But it gets better than that. The Talmud says that if we give the 10 percent commission to charities that are in congruence with the Divine purpose for the universe, we will make much more money in the future.

This is illustrated by the following Talmudic account. The great sage of the Talmud, Rabbi Meir (died circa 100 B.C.E.), is reported to have said (Kiddushin, 82a): "One should always teach his son a clean and easy craft, and pray to Him to whom all wealth and property belong [to God], because every craft contains the potentialities for both poverty and wealth. Neither poverty nor wealth is due to the craft, but all depends on merit."

How does one build merit in the sight of God to gain the blessing of increased wealth? As the Talmud states, mentioned above, praying is one way of gaining the said merit. However, there is another way to build the merit and blessing that brings wealth, and two Talmudic accounts shed light on this (Shabbat 119a and Ta'anit 9a). "Rebbe asked Rabbi Ishmael, son of Rabbi Jose, how do the wealthy in the Land of Israel merit their wealth? He replied it was because they give tithes, as it is written (Deuteronomy 14:22), *Asser te'asser*, meaning, give tithes ['*asser*] so that you may become wealthy [*tit'asser*]."

The Talmud relates another story that reinforces this point. Rabbi Yohanan asked his young nephew to recite the verse he learned from the Torah that day at school. The young lad replied with the verse that states, "Give tithes." He then asked his uncle, "What is the meaning of the words 'Give tithes?'" Rabbi Yohanan answered: "Give tithes so that you may become rich." The boy then asked, "Can you prove that you get rich by tithing?" Rabbi Yohanan replied: "Go and test it for yourself." The boy then asked: "Is it permitted to test God? Don't the scriptures say (Deuteronomy 6:16) that 'You shall not test God?'" Rabbi Yohanan replied, quoting another sage named Rabbi Oshaia: "The case of tithe-giving is excluded from the prohibition not to test God, as it is written (Malachi 3:10), 'Bring the whole tithe to the storehouse, that there may be food in My house, and test Me with this now, said the Lord of Hosts, [and see whether] I will not open for you the windows of heaven, and pour out more than enough blessing.'"

Clearly the Torah sees the concept of tithing as a guaranteed method of merit building that brings the blessing of wealth. According to the Torah, however, this does not mean that you must give the tithes to your place of worship. You may give the tithe directly to the poor or to any other worthy charity as well.

This idea encapsulates what spiritual entrepreneurs really are: people who see their charitable giving as an integral part of a business strategy towards success. They see their business as a conduit for God's blessing for wealth. They are passionate about being responsible stewards of that wealth. They understand that their business is another method by which they can connect to both a higher power and to others by making the world a better and more divinely sensitive place and by so doing make more money as well.

The spiritual entrepreneur is not just a selfish person who is using the giving of charity as a means to grow their fortune. Rather they see their charitable giving as a motivation for making money. The spiritual entrepreneur has an underlying ability to see beyond the external reality of the universe. Underlying all of existence, the mystics say, is a Divine energy that sustains it all.

The Divine is also known in Judaism as the *Ain Sof*, or the "Never-Ending." Since it has no end, it is therefore logical to say that it had no beginning either. When we meditate on this idea, we realize that since all physical things are dependent on the Divine energy for their subsistence, the true nature of everything is the Divine energy inherent within them. Divine energy is infinite. Being infinite means that there is no end to the amount of possibilities and opportunities that emanate from it.

Contrast this with the outer veneer that is called reality and the difference is dramatic. All of what is seen is able to be quantified. The house a person lives in has a definite square footage; the car they drive has a specific make, model, year, and color. All physical objects by definition are limited and can be measured. Conversely, the deeper layer of existence has no specifications. It is inherently infinite. If we are able to tap in to this level of existence, we are tapping into the layer where everything is possible.

This is the level on which spiritual entrepreneurs live their lives. They have real vision. They are able to see beyond the surface and into the deeper realm of reality. Because of this, they are able to see business as more than just a moneymaking game. They see their entrepreneurship as another avenue to achieve a higher and loftier goal. For them, money is not just a tool that brings them a higher standard of living. Money is not just there so that they can enjoy a new sports car or expensive vacation. It is there to allow a loftier vision to be fulfilled in this world.

This is not to say that spiritual entrepreneurs will not enjoy and indulge in the finer things life has to offer—they may. However, for them that is not the primary motivation of making money—it is a bonus. Their ability to see into the deeper realm of reality that contains infinite Divine energy allows them to view the moneymaking process in an enlightened manner. Because of this they are able to tap into the Divine energy which brings them financial success.

INSIGHT FOR BUSINESS: *Focus on the primary task, which is to make money. Remember, however, to set aside at least 10 percent of the money to make the world a better and more divine place. This approach is good for business because it attracts additional divine energy that brings more success in its stead.*

INSIGHT FOR LIFE: *Try to build your merit. This involves praying, giving to charity, and helping others. The more merit you are able to garner, the more Divine energy you attract and the more successful you will be in every area of life.*

LEV LEVIEV: A PROTOTYPE SPIRITUAL ENTREPRENEUR

America had Horatio Alger. Japan had Soichiro Honda. And Israel had Lev Leviev (before he moved to London in early 2008), who is now estimated to be worth a staggering $8 billion. As a teenager, he arrived in Israel with literally the rags on his back. He and his family escaped the Soviet region of Bukhara and reached Israel in 1971. He left high school after an attempt at rabbinical studies and entered the freewheeling world of diamond dealing. Israel is the world's capital of diamond cutting, and the city of Ramat Gan is the center of that industry. Leviev, along with many of his relatives, served as street dealers—trading diamonds to various cutting houses in the city.

It was a dangerous job, but it could be lucrative. Leviev soon was making a nice income from his diamond trading activities. But he wasn't satisfied. From a young age he knew he would be wealthy, and he was impatient to get there. According to a 2007 *New York Times* profile, he once told his friend and fellow street trader Paul Raps: "You know what we need? We need to get our hands on the *gelem*."

The *gelem* is Hebrew slang for uncut diamonds. Raps and his colleagues laughed at the notion. There was only one place to get the *gelem*, and that was De Beers, the powerful South African diamond cartel. They controlled the entire market and set the price according to their whim.

But Leviev had a plan. He returned to Russia during the Gorbachev era and convinced that country's government to take advantage of its diamond mines and challenge De Beers. Gorbachev was not long from falling from power, but Leviev kept his contacts in the Russian diamond industry and soon had created an international consortium to funnel Russian diamonds to the world markets. Through that process, he ended De Beers's monopoly on all diamond sales. He had gotten his hands on the *gelem*.

Leviev's relationships in Russia opened the door for him to establish a company in Angola. That African country had vast diamond reserves that had yet to be exploited due to a long civil war. But Leviev arrived just as the civil war was ending, and he soon established a joint distribution contract between his company and the government of Angola.

Along the way, Leviev did something that most budding tycoons do not: he began to give away his fortune. His goal was to tithe 10 percent of his income every year, but he soon found himself giving far more than that. Some years it was 20 percent. Other years it was 30 percent. He founded Jewish day schools in the former Soviet states. He paid the salaries of hundreds of outreach rabbis in the former Soviet Union. His latest goal is to provide a free Jewish education for any American Jewish child who wants one. Former Soviet dissident and current Israeli politician Natan Sharansky says of Leviev: "I know a lot of rich people who give money. But Leviev is on a completely different level. He's building entire communities."

In early 2008, Leviev made headlines worldwide by purchasing a London house for more than $70 million. The British tabloids detailed the extravagance of the home: its swimming pools, gardens, and elaborate stone staircase. The tone of the stories seemed to be asking: "Who does this arrogant man think he is?" When Leviev was asked about this by Israeli business publication *Globes,* he responded, "I don't like to talk about my private affairs. Our modesty is measured in our good deeds and in the conduct of the company."

This mirrors the Torah perspective on such a purchase. Leviev is a man who has donated more money to charity, both in sum total and in percentage amount, than most of the other wealthiest people in the world. His business, according to him, is to make money, but he does so in order to be able to serve God better. But God does not ask that more than a 10 or 20 percent commission be paid to charity. This Leviev does in an exemplary fashion. He has been blessed with riches because he is a responsible steward of that blessing and he has every right to enjoy the rest of the money in any ethical and legal way he likes. Instead of being jealous of his new home, people should learn from Lev Leviev's spiritual entrepreneurship and recognize the benefits it brings.

The Benefits of Spiritual Entrepreneurship

There are numerous other benefits of spiritual entrepreneurship. First, as mentioned in Chapter 2, our deepest human desires represent two elements: connecting with others and connecting with something higher. Spiritual entrepreneurship does both. Using the money made from business to support good causes that help others is, according to the Torah, an act that connects us to something higher.

Giving to charity is a *mitzvah,* an action that the Torah mandates. The word *mitzvah* has two etymologies. One is the word *tzav,* which means "to command." In this sense a *mitzvah* is a commandment of God. But, the mystics say, it also comes from the word *tzafsa,* which means "connecting." Doing a *mitzvah* connects us to God. So our very acts of giving charity to a worthy cause connect us with something higher than ourselves. This is in addition to the fact that giving charity connects the donors with others—the recipients—as well. Clearly, spiritual entrepreneurs are able to achieve true satisfaction and fulfillment by making their charitable giving a focal point of their business.

There's another advantage to spiritual entrepreneurship. It allows the entrepreneur to focus on what business is really all about—making money. It is common for wealthy people, of the classic entrepreneurial type, to feel a sense of guilt over their financial success. An example of this is Warren Buffett. In an interview with Ben Stein in the *New*

York Times, published on November 26, 2006, he talked about his discomfort with being as wealthy as he is. As Stein wrote:

> Mr. Buffett compiled a data sheet of the men and women who work in his office. He had each of them make a fraction; the numerator was how much they paid in federal income tax and in payroll taxes for Social Security and Medicare, and the denominator was their taxable income. The people in his office were mostly secretaries and clerks, though not all.
>
> It turned out that Mr. Buffett, with immense income from dividends and capital gains, paid far, far less as a fraction of his income than the secretaries or the clerks or anyone else in his office. Further, in conversation it came up that Mr. Buffett doesn't use any tax planning at all. He just pays as the Internal Revenue Code requires. "How can this be fair?" he asked of how little he pays relative to his employees. "How can this be right?"
>
> Even though I agreed with him, I warned that whenever someone tried to raise the issue, he or she was accused of fomenting class warfare.
>
> "There's class warfare, all right," Mr. Buffett said, "but it's my class, the rich class, that's making war, and we're winning."

Or, as Mr. Buffett later said at a $4,600-a-seat fundraiser in New York for Senator Hillary Clinton, "The 400 of us [here] pay a lower part of our income in taxes than our receptionists do, or our cleaning ladies, for that matter. If you're in the luckiest one percent of humanity, you owe it to the rest of humanity to think about the other 99 percent."

Let us call this Rich Guilt. It is not uncommon amongst the self-made wealthy. The guilt stems from the fact that while they are very comfortable, others continue to suffer around them. In addition, they feel that they are just making money and not contributing to others in a meaningful way. Mr. Buffett, for example, did not start really giving money to charity until he was seventy-six, when he gave ten million shares of his company's stock to the Bill & Melinda Gates Foundation. That single donation was worth approximately $30.7 billion at the time. Up to that point, his entire life was dedicated to one pursuit: making money. And he was extremely successful at it. But in the end he realized that all it brought him was guilt. Although he denied this guilt, his own words, published in *Warren Buffett Speaks* by Janet Lowe (Wiley, 1997), the guilt shines through:

> I work in a market system that happens to reward what I do very well—disproportionately well. Mike Tyson, too. If you can knock a guy out in 10 seconds and earn $10 million for it, this world will pay a lot for that. If you can bat .360, this world will pay a lot for that. If you're a marvelous teacher, this world won't pay a lot for it. If you are a terrific nurse, this world will not pay a lot for it.

One can argue that Warren Buffett was feeling guilty of being part of an injustice that paid him so well for doing a job that was not any more important than that of a teacher or nurse. So, at the age of seventy-six, he decided to donate most of his wealth to charity.

Spiritual entrepreneurs have no such guilt, because they never see their business as a means to make more money for themselves. For the spiritual entrepreneur, wealth creation is about making the world a better and more Godly place. They therefore give at least 10 percent of their income to charity. They do this as they earn the money and not when they reach old age. Distinct from classic entrepreneurs like Buffett, spiritual entrepreneurs do not think that because the rich give a smaller percentage of their income back to society in the way of taxes, the government should raise their tax rate. The reason for this is clear: spiritual entrepreneurs are voluntarily giving back to society a larger percentage of their income than most middle-class people do through their taxes.

Our prototype spiritual entrepreneur Lev Leviev, in a *New York Times* article published in 2007, described his attitude towards philanthropy as opposed to others such as Warren Buffet: "A lot of very rich men wait too long to give their money away," he said. "Warren Buffett, for example. He's in his seventies now, and he should have started earlier. But Bill Gates is a young man, and he's already giving to help the world. That's the right way to do it." What Lev Leviev was describing was one of the defining differences between classic entrepreneurs and what we have termed spiritual entrepreneurs.

> **INSIGHT FOR BUSINESS:** *By making charitable giving a focal part of your financial plans, you are constantly giving back to society, making the experience of being rich more enjoyable and making you less prone to guilt.*

> **INSIGHT FOR LIFE:** *In everything you do there is the opportunity to give and take. Whenever you take, you must try to give as well.*

Turning Your Business into Your Own Personal Place of Worship

There is little doubt that the type of entrepreneur we become affects the way we feel about doing business. We spend most of the waking day pursuing a livelihood. If we were able to sanctify that process it would be immensely beneficial—it would make the entire process more fulfilling and therefore more enjoyable. The concept here is rather simple. According to the great mystics, the intention is central. In fact, according to some of the great Torah sages, the intention takes precedence over the act itself. For example, a prayer which is done without proper intention is meaningless. Intention sometimes even trumps action.

By taking a material object and intending to use it for the purposes that God intended, we are elevating that object and placing it on the spiritual sphere. Consider a piece of cheesecake. If we eat the cake out of gluttony and concentrate only on how much pleasure the taste gives us, we have done nothing but add more sugar and fat to our bodies. But if we eat the cake having in mind how we are going to use the energy it gives us to do a good deed, we have sanctified and elevated the eating of that piece of cake. Analogously, if we go to the gym to remain healthy so that we can better pray or help others, and we think about that while we exercise, we have sanctified the experience. In a similar manner, if while doing business, we consciously have in mind that we will use at least 10 percent of the money to make the world a better or more God-conscious place, we have converted our workplace into a place of worship. And the Torah promises us that doing so will increase our wealth.

INSIGHT FOR BUSINESS: *Going to work can be as fulfilling as going to a place of worship. In fact, by becoming a spiritual entrepreneur you become the minister of your own place of worship—your business. This way the moneymaking process is invigorated with a divine spirit. This is easy to fulfill as well as incredibly rewarding.*

INSIGHT FOR LIFE: *As you add spirituality to your life, keep in mind that the power of intent is very potent. Whatever you do should have an underlying purpose that goes beyond the selfish and narcissistic quest for more pleasure. Realizing this will imbue every aspect of your life with more spirituality.*

Meditation

The idea underlying spiritual entrepreneurship is that all things can be imbued with spirituality if they are motivated by a higher purpose. Contemplative meditation is vital to making this concept work, because it can help motivate you and ensure that your intention for a higher purpose remains constant.

Think about your particular business and what motivates you to pursue it. Ask yourself whether you have a higher purpose for it. If the answer is yes, then try and contemplate what that purpose is and whether you are actually pursuing it. As you contemplate, use the steps of meditation outlined in the Appendix to reconnect with it.

If your purpose does not lie beyond making money to satisfy your immediate selfish and self-serving needs and desires, begin contemplating on why it is important to have a higher purpose. Consider the difference between the three types of entrepreneurs discussed in this chapter. Use the steps found in the Appendix to connect with why it is beneficial to become a spiritual entrepreneur. Once you feel that you have really connected to that idea, think about what higher purpose you want to achieve with the money you make from your business. Now that you have decided what that purpose will be, we welcome you into the club of spiritual entrepreneurs.

CHAPTER 8

THINK GOOD

Harnessing the Power of Positivity
to Realize Your Goals

Think Good and it will be good.

—THE TZEMECH TZEDEK

DAVID EINHORN, FAMOUS ON WALL STREET FOR ALWAYS BEING INvolved in "doom and gloom" stocks, attributes a great deal of his own success to his optimism. According to the thirty-nine-year-old Einhorn, positive thinking is most potent if a person engages in optimism at a time when most of the rest of the world is indulging in pessimism.

Einhorn is known as one of the gurus of an investment philosophy called value investing. And he's been very successful at it. The hedge fund that he manages, Greenlight Capital, Inc., has more than $5 billion in assets. The theory behind value investing is, as its name implies, finding value where others don't.

The founder of this school of investing, Benjamin Graham, admitted that the stock market tends to do relatively well at determining the proper valuation of companies. But if you want to beat the market, Graham pointed out, you have to find investments where the market has made a temporary mistake in its valuation. Such mistakes will always be rectified with time, he preached. So, according to Graham, the key to beating the market is to invest in stocks whose prices are lower than they should be.

Sounds easy, right? The difficulty, as Einhorn and other investors who play this game tell us, is that when the rest of the world is convinced that a stock stinks, sticking with it is always a test of intestinal fortitude. "You have to believe that your convictions are correct," says Einhorn, adding: "You've got to believe that things will get better with time."

And that fundamental belief in progress is the foundation for Einhorn's optimism. Anyone who doesn't believe that lifespans will increase over the next fifty years, incomes will rise, and the standard of living of most people will improve, shouldn't buy stocks. In other words, Einhorn believes, every stock purchase is an act of optimism.

Einhorn's specialty, however, is out-of-favor stocks—which takes a much stronger form of positive thinking. "It's pretty easy to be optimistic about a stock which has already doubled or tripled and nobody can find a thing wrong with it," he says. Staying with a value stock, on the other hand, is what separates the hardcore optimist from the fair-weather positive thinker.

He cites one of his most successful investments as an example: Freescale Semiconductor. The maker of cell phone chips used to be a business unit of tech giant Motorola. But that company was being pushed by shareholders to concentrate on its other, larger businesses. So it spun off Freescale in an Initial Public Offering in the summer of 2004.

The IPO was a disaster. Right before it went to market, Motorola had to lower its price dramatically in order to keep the deal alive. The stock market didn't seem to want to have anything to do with an unwanted part of another company—the share price didn't budge for about six months.

The biggest participant in the IPO was David Einhorn's Greenlight fund. At one point, a large chunk of the fund's money was invested in this company that nobody else wanted. "Everyone else saw a phone chip company with unexciting prospects," Einhorn says. "We saw a company that made a lot of different chips that had a lot of growth in front of them. Their chips went in appliances, in automobiles, and in other things."

In addition, Einhorn was convinced that the new company's independence would cause it to grow. "They had been forced to do too many pet projects for Motorola," he says. "As an independent company they could concentrate on growth alone."

Throughout the fall of 2004, Einhorn's optimism about the company was tested on a daily basis. The stock moved up and down in little spurts, but it wasn't shooting up the way he thought it deserved to do. Every day, he reviewed his assumptions about the stock to make sure they were still valid. And every day, his judgment stayed true. "You always have to be asking yourself: 'Am I being patient, or am I being stubborn?'" Einhorn says. The trick to knowing the difference is when fundamental changes happen. "If I find myself inventing a new reason for why the investment is still sound, I know it's time to pull out and start with something new."

Then things took off with Freescale. Their earnings kept growing and the stock started moving. Then it started skyrocketing as others realized its growth potential. In 2006, the company was bought by a group led by Blackstone, one of the largest private equity companies in the world. The selling price was for $17 billion, nearly triple what the company was valued when Einhorn had bought into it. That year, his fund had a 26 percent return.

To Einhorn, it was all about optimism. Without a firm resolve in the positive outcome of his investment, he could have easily pulled out of the stock earlier—and accepted the pessimism of the rest of the market about Freescale. But Einhorn's belief in a brighter future won out.

Success Begins with Optimism

Clearly, thoughtful optimism breeds success. Take a room full of CEOs, millionaires, and others who have reached the pinnacle of their goals, and you'll almost certainly find a room full of people who are, by their nature, optimistic and positive.

There are plenty of explanations for why that is true. Some claim it is because positive-minded people are cheerful and fun to be around, and are therefore chosen over negative people when it comes time to win the contract or make the sale. Others, like Einhorn, believe that it is just part of a good investment and business strategy. Yet others say that it's a fundamental law of the universe (often referred to as "the law of attraction").

While not discounting the former two theories, the Torah seems to support the third thesis as well. While it offers no mathematical formula that proves it, anecdotal evidence abounds. Torah teachings stress optimism and positive thinking as keys to attracting success and positive outcomes. At the same time, the Torah also stresses that thought itself will not accomplish anything. It is only when thought is combined with action that positive thinking can result in the realization of dreams and the bringing of success.

The Power of Positive Language and How to Harness It

The idea that positive thinking results in positive outcomes can be traced back to the story of Noah and the Flood in Genesis. The Torah generally calls kosher animals *tahor* (pure) and non-kosher animals *tamay* (which means "impure," but also brings with it connotations of unholiness and immorality). However, in the famous story of Noah and the flood, where a sample of all animals entered the Noah's ark to take refuge from the massive floodwaters, the Torah says (Genesis 7:2): "From all *tahor* animals and from the animals which are not *tahor*." In this case the Torah desists from using the word *tamay*, which has more negative implications, and instead refers to the *tamay* animals as "not *tahor*." The Torah does this even though it is generally careful not to use additional words—in this case three extra words—unless it wants the reader to learn something from them. The Talmud (Pesachim 3a) explains that the reason for the reluctance to use the word *tamay* in this story is to teach us not to use words in the negative construction (to avoid the additional connotations) even if it means using additional words in a sentence. Simply stated, the Torah is trying to teach us to speak in the positive rather than the negative.

The Talmud commentators note that when the Torah discusses laws—and clarity is an absolute priority—it uses the word *tamay* many times. However, when it is relating "stories," it uses additional words to say things in the positive. This is because words have power, and when we says something negative we are attracting that same negative thing towards ourselves. The Torah teaches us to use words that do not have negative connotations so that they do not bring negativity into our lives. Since a person's words come from their thoughts, the mind is the source of our positive or negative language. The opposite is also true: our words influence our thoughts. Speaking what's on our minds gives permanence to our thoughts. In addition, when we talk about something, more thoughts about the same subject will appear. Since words have such power it is vitally important that our words reflect a positive attitude. And it is equally important that our thoughts—the source of our words—are positive. We should therefore replace our negative thoughts with positive ones so that we can attract positivity to ourselves.

The power of positive thinking—and by extension positive speech—has been reiterated by the great Jewish mystics. The great Hasidic master and Kabbalist Rabbi Nachman of Breslov (whom we met in Chapter 1) said: "If you believe that you can ruin, then believe that you can fix." In other words, instead of focusing on the negative, concentrate on the positive, using your mental resources to repair things rather than to damage them.

The best example of the suggested use of the power of positive thinking taught by Torah sages, however, comes from the great Kabbalist and Hasidic Master known as the the Tzemech Tzedek (1789-1866). Once asked to pray on behalf of a seriously ill person, he responded telling the family to practice positive thinking. He advised, in Yiddish, "*Tracht gut vet zain gut,*" meaning "Think good and it will be good." Many people assume that this is some sort of wishful thinking, but consider for a moment whether you have ever heard someone who is very successful in their line of work speak pessimistically. Think, too, about the person you know who always complains that things aren't going right. Almost always, you will find that successful people don't focus on the negative, while unsuccessful people often do.

You might say that this is because a successful person has nothing to complain about, but this would be untrue: even the richest among us has known sorrow and loss and disappointment. In this chapter, however, we put forth the proposition that people's positive attitude is a primary reason for their attraction of success and accomplishments.

INSIGHT FOR BUSINESS: *Positive thinking is the hallmark of a successful businessperson. By being positive you will attract positive outcomes to your business.*

INSIGHT FOR LIFE: *Positive speech and positive thinking will attract positive things into your life.*

Success Doesn't End with Positive Thinking

Despite the truism that positive thoughts and positive speech attract positivity into our lives, we would be naive to think that this is all we need to succeed. It is important to understand that while positive thinking is vital, it by itself is not *the* secret to realizing success.

In this regard there are two types of people. The first might be called the "Big Talkers." These people think and talk positively but do not actually go out and actively do what it takes to make their dreams come true. The other type is made up of the "Big Doers." These people have a positive outlook and tremendous faith in their abilities but also work intelligently to make their dreams come true. These are the people who will actually succeed.

The Big Talker is represented by the old joke about Jack. Every day, Jack begs God to deliver him from his poverty by allowing him to win the lottery. After receiving no response from his repeated prayers, Jack cries out to God: "Why won't you answer my prayers?" Amidst thunder and smoke, a frustrated God responds, "Jack! Meet me halfway! Buy a lottery ticket!"

Although we may recognize that when we think positive thoughts we are attracting positive outcomes, if we do not stretch out our hands to grab them, the positive outcomes will pass us by. This is what the sages meant when they said (Song of Songs, Rabbah 5:2) that our obligation is to open the door just a little and then God will push it open the rest of the way. But if we don't initiate the opening of the door, it will remain closed.

This is also what the mystics meant when they said that is it necessary to make a *kli* (vessel) to catch the blessings that rain down upon us. The Divine energy of the universe, otherwise known as God, sends us blessings when we ask for them. However, we must do our part as well and prepare a vessel to receive the goodness that we have attracted. Often, people don't make the vessel, and as a result the positive energy they have attracted is unable to actually enter their lives. It remains on the periphery, waiting for something tangible—a *kli*—so that it can manifest.

In addition, the sages tell us in the Talmud (Megila 6b) that people who say that they succeeded without hard work are not to be believed. People who say that they worked hard but did not succeed are similarly not to be believed. But people who say that they worked hard and succeeded should be believed. Clearly, positive action—hard work—is required in addition to positive thought and speech that bring Divine blessings.

> **INSIGHT FOR BUSINESS:** *Hard work is a prerequisite for success in business. Don't make the mistake of thinking that positive thoughts alone will bring you new clients or improve your bottom line. Positive thought and speech must be coupled with positive action in order to realize your financial goals.*

> **INSIGHT FOR LIFE:** *Positive thinking alone will not get you anywhere. It must be paired with actual deeds if real success is to be achieved in any area of life.*

How Positive Thinking Attracts Positive Consequences

The mind is the highest and most spiritual faculty of the human body, says the Kabbalah. According to Maimonides (1138-1204), one of the greatest Jewish philosophers and jurists of all time, our intellect is the best conduit for connecting with the Divine. He saw the human mind as intimately connected with what he termed the "Active Intellect," also known as the "Divine Intellect"—a Divine attribute that is independent of the human being. Maimonides believed that all of our thoughts are influenced by the Active, or Divine, Intellect. The relationship between the Divine Intellect and the human intellect goes both ways. Just as the Divine Intellect is the source of our thoughts, our minds can also attract energy from the Divine Intellect.

The Divine Intellect is the energy behind all of existence. In Genesis, it is stated that God created the world using ten sayings, each of which begins with the words "And God said":

1. "Let there be light."
2. "Let there be . . . waters."
3. "Let . . . the dry land appear."
4. "Let the land put forth . . . fruit trees . . ."
5. "Let there be lights to divide the day from the night . . ."
6. "Let the birds fly above the land . . ."
7. "Let the earth bring forth . . . cattle, creeping things, and animals . . ."
8. "Let us make man in our image . . ."
9. "Be fruitful, and multiply . . ."
10. "I have given you . . . food."

The Kabbalists take this notion that God created the universe with sayings to mean that His speech was the tool He used to create and to sustain the universe. In this sense God's speech is used as a metaphor for the energy that created and now sustains all that exists. Speech is a revelation of our thoughts. The Divine speech that created the world is no different—within each of the ten sayings used by God to create the universe are His thoughts. So within God's creative energy that we have termed His speech is a more profound Divine energy that we have called His thoughts or the Divine Intellect. In other words the true makeup of the universes creative energy is the Divine Intellect. However, we cannot relate to others through our thoughts—for this we need speech. God also used what we have termed speech—

not thought—to create the world, because He was relating to the universe and not to Himself (allegorically speaking). Since speech is the manifestation of thoughts, when the Kabbalists say that God's speech sustains the universe, they are in fact saying that His thoughts give energy to the universe. So when we, using our thoughts, connect to the Divine Intellect we are, in fact, connecting to the energy that keeps the universe and all its aspects in existence.

To get a better handle on this, we must understand that the physical outer veneer of existence is only a small amount of what really exists. According to the mystics, there are layers of existence that are neither material nor mundane. Modern physics backs up this concept. When reduced to the smallest possible building block (subatomic particles) matter behaves like waves of energy. But when we pick up a coffee cup, we don't see waves. Our senses are fooling us into thinking that the coffee cup is a discrete piece of solid material, when a physicist would explain that it's actually a bunching of energy within a broader fabric of energy.

A mystic would have a similar perspective as the physicist, although the mystic would see it in a more abstract fashion. The mystic senses beyond the waves of energy and sees through to the Divine energy inherent in all things.

This is why the great Jewish mystics were also great meditators. Meditation is—at its most fundamental level—the ability to focus your thoughts in the direction you desire. Mystics, for example, want to connect directly with the Divine. They do this by directing their thoughts to think about the deeper Divine reality that exists beyond the physical veneer of the universe. As they do this, they connect with that reality which we have also called the Divine Intellect. They are thus able to bring real divinity into their lives and live on a higher realm. When they do this, the laws of nature governing the outer veneer of reality cease to have a direct impact on their lives and they see miracles manifest. You can use this technique to achieve greater success in business. By contemplating the underlying Divine energy that animates and sustains all of creation, you can tap into that energy. If you see the world on that level of reality and are able to think deeply about attracting that energy into your life, it will come. On that level anything is possible and all things can be attracted—provided, of course, that the other elements—positive speech and positive action—are also in play.

Similarly, however, since our intellect and thoughts interact directly with the Divine Intellect when we think positive thoughts and speak in a positive manner, we are able to attract positivity into our lives. This provides the businessperson with an additional benefit, for the act of positive speech often leads to other satisfying rewards. In business, you are more often judged by the words that come out of your mouth than by anything else. When those words are released amidst negativity and pessimism, you are judged by the people around you as being negative. But if you can bring yourself to phrase words in a positive context and refrain from negative speech, you will notice a change in the way people respond to you.

This does not mean that you always have to be bright and cheerful and avoid criticizing your peers. The content of your words is important. But the method you use to verbalize your thoughts can be just as significant. Relaying bad news or couching necessary criticism in positive language can go a long way to making that person your friend rather than your enemy. Positivity has many bonuses.

INSIGHT FOR BUSINESS: *Your mind is able to tap directly into the most potent energy available. Make use of this ability to attract profitable opportunities for your business.*

INSIGHT FOR LIFE: *Realize there is a reality that is deeper than the surface. Connecting to the Divine reality is easier than you may have thought and will bring immeasurable benefits in its wake.*

The Positive Power of Intention

The Torah prizes intention to the extent that some sages say it has an even higher value than action. And although prayer has a central place in the religion, the sages say that prayer without intention is like a bird that has a body but no wings—it will never achieve its goal, and is thus ineffective. Saying the words of prayer without emotional feeling makes the prayer unsuccessful and the requests go unanswered. In light of what we have said above, this is easily understood. The energy that we transmit through positive thoughts and emotions comes into contact with its counterpart, Divine energy, and attracts positive energy in return. If, however, we pray without any feeling, intention, or thought, the energy has not been transmitted and will not attract the Divine energy. Prayer also underlines the need for positive words to go with the positive thoughts. Since, as mentioned previously, words give permanence to thoughts, to be most effective, audible verbalized prayer is necessary. The words make it easier for our positivity, which in this case manifests as petitional prayer, to reach the target: Divine energy.

This concept doesn't just hold true about prayer. The power of intention is important if you are to attract positive things into your business and life. To do this, you must make a list of the things you want to attract and then use the power of intention to think deeply about them. Visualizing the positive things you want to attract is a great way to use the power of intention. However, together with this, positive speech is needed. You should both intend and visualize the desired situation, but if you talk negatively about obtaining it, it may never come. In addition, positive speech regarding the things you want to obtain gives permanence and potency to the positive energy transmitted, making it easier to attract the desired things.

INSIGHT FOR BUSINESS: *Intention is vital. Use the power of intention to visualize the new project or venture you are trying to create and attract it to yourself. At the same time, make sure that you are talking in a positive manner about attracting and achieving the things you use your power of intention to attract.*

INSIGHT FOR LIFE: *Remember to be careful with your words. Positive words will attract positive outcomes and the opposite is also true.*

The Positive Power of Gratitude

Another important aspect to positive thought is the concept of gratitude. Upon waking up in the morning, traditional Jews will say blessings thanking God for everything in life. In fact, the first thing that is supposed to be said in the morning is a short prayer of gratitude, thanking God for returning our soul and for giving us a new day. The next step is to bless God for clothing us and providing all the other necessities of life.

This has a double effect. First, it makes us feel grateful for everything that is already in our lives. And the mere fact that we are alive and well, and have food and a roof, means that we already have abundance. Second, by blessing God and showing gratitude for those necessities, we demonstrate a realization of the Divine Intellect that has supplied such abundance.

The power of gratitude is beautifully demonstrated for us in a classic tract from the Torah's oral law that gives advice for life. In Ethics of the Fathers (4:1) the sages ask: "Who is wealthy?" The answer given is that the person who is happy with his or her portion is wealthy.

A common interpretation of the meaning of this passage is that even if you are poor but are satisfied with what you have in life, you can be considered wealthy. On a literal level, this might seem absurd, because real financial wealth only comes to the person who pursues it. If you are satisfied being poor you will never pursue wealth. And if wealth is truly defined by the level of satisfaction a person has, then wealth has no correlation to money and is therefore an inaccurate definition of the word.

There is, however, another way of looking at this. The question the Torah sages may have been really asking is this: What type of person has the potential to achieve real *financial* wealth? The answer is that it is only the person who is truly happy (rather than "satisfied") with what he or she currently has. (Note that the term used by the sages is *sameach,* which means "happy," rather then the word *soveah* which would mean "satisfied.") There is a difference between being happy and being satisfied. We can be happy but not satisfied. Happiness is a state of being and satisfaction is a state of mind. We can be happy with what we have but still not be satisfied with it. Having aspirations for more does not mean that we cannot be happy with what we have—it is just that we want more for the future. When we are satisfied, however, we do not want more. We feel as we do after a big meal: we cannot think about more food. In short, if you are *satisfied* with what you have achieved you will not be motivated to achieve more. You can, however, be *happy* with what you have achieved and still want to achieve more.

There is however even more depth here. The sages may be saying that *only* a person who is happy, and therefore gives thanks for what he or she currently has, can become truly wealthy. The logic is simple. People who are miserable will tap into energy that brings them misery; sad vibes will attract more sadness. In addition, if we are merely satisfied with what we have, we will give out a vibe that says that we don't want anything else, therefore not attracting more of what we already have into our lives. But if we are happy and therefore feel gratitude for what we have, we will always want more of the same. That energy will meet its counterpart in the Divine energy and will therefore bring us more of that happy and appreciative energy, which in turn will bring more of what we currently have. This is why the sages say that only people who are happy with what they currently have will be able to attract real wealth into their lives.

Gratitude also has another very important value in the business world, especially if you can apply it to the people with whom you work. The employee review process, for instance, is universally loathed by employees. That's because it all too often centers on negative criticism. But the vast majority of employees are indeed doing a good job (they would have been fired if they weren't), so a more constructive approach is to structure an employee review around the positive attributes of that employee and showing gratitude for the work that they have done for the business. Negative work habits should be mentioned as an important aside that needs to be repaired, but they should not take center stage in the review process. Ultimately, gratitude for employees by their bosses will awaken within the employee the desire to do even more for their company. This is analogous to how gratitude in general awakens positive Divine energy towards the thankful person.

A frequent mistake that managers make is to avoid giving credit to those they supervise when given a forum to do so. Many managers instead take opportunities such as award banquets or company meetings to praise their own superiors, thinking that such words of praise will advance their own careers. Based on what we have discussed, a better way of approaching such situations is for the manager to use such opportunities to praise those who have worked well under them—because if it were not for the successful execution of their responsibilities, the manager would not be in a position to thank anyone. Like positive speech, being grateful pays off in more ways than one.

INSIGHT FOR BUSINESS: *Being* satisfied *with what you have is never good for business because it causes complacency. Being* happy *with what you have, however, is vital for success. Remember also to always show gratitude to employees, business associates, and to God.*

INSIGHT FOR LIFE: *Be happy. Misery begets misery. Happiness attracts more of the same. This is as true for relationships as it is for business. Happiness will attract happy relationships.*

The Negative Power of Doubt

The great Master Rabbi Israel Baal Shem Tov (1698–1760) was one of the greatest Jewish mystics ever to live and the founder of modern Hasidic Judaism. His father died when he was a young boy. The last words the young Israel heard from his father was, "Fear nothing but God." He took these words to heart, and using them as the basis for his philosophy on life he was able to achieve unrivaled greatness and success. He has influenced the lives of millions and his philosophy and outlook lives on in the lives of millions till this very day. Without fear, Rabbi Israel Baal Shem Tov was free from worry and he lived without doubt, which is a product of fear. He went ahead with what he knew had to be done and pursued his vision fearlessly, with the faith that it would all come to be. With this he was able to succeed in becoming the founder of Hasidism, one of the most successful movements in Judaism.

While the concept of fear has been dealt with elsewhere in this book, here we will focus on one of its derivatives: doubt. If we are fearless, there is no reason for doubt—we just go forward and do what needs to be done. If we are afraid of change or of what the future might bring then we often begin to have irrational fear-based reservations about making the changes at all. Doubt transmits negative energy that can sabotage the process of attaining goals. If you say, "I really would like to win this contract, but I doubt that I will," or "I would love to attract that client but I fear that my business is too small," the negative energy of that doubt will attract its negative counterpart in the Divine energy and will become a self-fulfilling prophecy. This is why the overcoming our fear is so important with regard to the power of positive thinking. The less we fear, the easier it is to be positive about outcomes. The more positive we are, the more good we attract into our lives and more successful we become.

Besides the fact that doubt begets negative energy, it is simply bad for business. Few things can cripple a business enterprise more than doubt, especially if that enterprise is structured so that middle managers are rewarded for maintaining the status quo and punished for taking risks. The antidote for doubt in a business setting is knowledge combined with hope. If you are advocating a daring action on the part of your firm, do not allow yourself to be defeated in discussions by the all-too-common response of "What if it doesn't work?" Instead, lay out a vision of how your plan will work, based on knowledge and information. And use all of your positive thinking skills to imbue your argument with the passion of hope. "Colleagues always respect real passion when they encounter it," says Kenneth Abramowitz, a founding partner of NGN Capital, a healthcare venture capital fund with more than $300 million under management. "But if you are passionate about something and then lack the knowledge about it to answer their questions with hard facts, they'll always overrule you."

INSIGHT FOR BUSINESS: *One of the traits most successful business-people have in common is that they have little or no doubt. When you see an opportunity that makes sense, pursue it fearlessly and never allow irrational doubts to throw you off course. Remember* *that doubt will interrupt the attraction of positive energy from the Divine Intellect.*

INSIGHT FOR LIFE: *Self-doubt will keep you from going forward with your dreams. It will also deflect success from you in every area where doubt resides.*

Beating the Negative Feelings

There is another source of negative energy besides doubt that must be countered: depression. What happens when a person is depressed and cannot seem to shake off that negative feeling? Waking up in the morning to a downbeat feeling is hard to change. Through meditation you may be able to push the negative thoughts away and replace them, at least temporarily, with positive ones. Instead of articulating the negative position of, for example, "I do not want X to happen," you can train yourself to say it in the affirmative, "I want Y to happen," or instead of using the word "bad," one may say "not good." However, deep down, the negative feeling remains and it is this that needs to be changed, because that deep-seated pessimism is the source of the negativity and will attract the same from the Divine Intellect.

The solution both is, and is not, simple. All you need to do is change your self-perception—easier said than done. You must come to see yourself as complete *as you are.* Not as your mother wishes you to be, not as the Joneses might measure you, not as the Superhero cum Business Mogul you might wish to be. You must see yourself as complete, just exactly as you are. To achieve this sense of completeness, you must be sincere with yourself. You must relate to yourself on a deeper plane, on the level of your soul.

Do not measure your success and failure against your external achievements. The true extent of success is deeply personal, and as we pointed out in Chapter 6, no two people measure it in the same way. But to be truly cognizant of this, you must be connected to yourself on a deeply personal, intimate, and authentic level. You will have to peel away all the artificial barriers that you have built around yourself for protection. You must see yourself for who you really are—a complete individual with no need for outside recognition to make you whole.

When you get in touch with your authentic self, on the level of your soul, you will see that, despite the fact that you can always improve outer elements of yourself, you are complete by virtue of the fact that you exist. This is the journey upon which the Kabbalists embark to see the deeper reality of the universe. You can see the world on the external artificial level where all that counts is the material. Or you can peel away the external and stare directly at the Divine energy (the Divine Intellect) that keeps all things in existence. When this is done, because there is nothing loftier than the Divine itself, the material loses its relevance.

People who see themselves on this deeper level become relaxed and comfortable with their place in life. Try the following exercise to illustrate how this works. Think about yourself and all your accomplishments. Ask yourself how you felt when you achieved each success in life. Now ask yourself if your accomplishments are you. If you hadn't gotten that promotion, would you still be the same person? If you hadn't finished your degree, would you still be the same person? Of course you would. The accomplishments or titles themselves are not part of who you really are deep down. They are merely garments of the material world that you wear.

When you take those garments off, what are you? Are you your body? The answer is, of course, no. We are far more than our physical conglomeration of proteins, cells, and organs. So now ask yourself again, what are you? The answer must be something else, something that lies deep inside you.

In Torah-speak, that something is called the soul, but you may call it energy or any other name that you want. On this level, ask yourself whether you feel complete. What else does your soul need to feel accomplished? If you have really gotten in contact with yourself on that deep level you should feel complete by virtue of the fact that you are alive. The soul does not need any external or physical additives to be content and fulfilled.

When you recognize that you really are your soul, you will begin to see external measurements of success are irrelevant. You will begin to feel good about yourself and your situation and you will have shed your negative thoughts and feelings.

But this "simple" process is not easy. You may have to go through it again and perhaps yet again, each time reaching deeper within. Once you feel secure in your own skin, however, you will be able to think and feel totally positive. You will no longer be encumbered by self-doubt or by comparing yourself to others.

The benefits of this strategy are twofold. First, life becomes more relaxed. Second, the positive and optimistic outlook and feeling that has been achieved actually helps attract the good things you want for your business or life.

This offers real wisdom and advice for the businessperson. It is important to realize that while money is often the barometer of business success, it cannot be the main goal. In every business, the goal must be to make the enterprise successful and since no two enterprises are exactly the same, the definition of success is unique for each business. By not trying to compare your business success with the successes of others, you can be much happier and optimistic about your own businesses achievements—thus attracting more of the same to the business.

INSIGHT FOR BUSINESS: *Recognize that your negative feelings are not allowing you to attract the things you need to achieve real success in your business and enterprise. Whenever negative or pessimistic feelings arise, remember this and dispel the negativity.*

INSIGHT FOR LIFE: *There is much more to life than competing with your neighbors, friends, and relatives. Remember to look inside when you seek peace of mind and positive feelings.*

Is Your Inside in Sync with Your Outside?

There is however, an additional problem that can deter us from attracting positivity from the Divine Intellect: we often fool ourselves. We act happy, so we think we are happy. We act loving, so we think that we feel loving. We act friendly, so we think that we feel friendly. But often the way we act is not the way we actually feel. In the West, where it is deemed to be unsociable to be miserable around others, many people never reveal their real feelings to other people. Although this may be based on a desire not to upset others with our negative feelings, this dual state of being is far from ideal and may even be harmful.

In the Talmud (Brachot 28a) there is a story of the ancient Jewish leader, Rabban Gamliel, who did not allow students who he determined were inauthentic into the house of study. The Talmud states that Gamliel only allowed the students whose "inside was like their outside" to enter the house of study. Having your inside in sync with your outside is considered a very important trait. But it doesn't mean that if you feel angry or sad you should just show it to the world. Rather it is saying that if you show happiness on the outside then it is important to feel it on the inside as well. Gamliel was referring to those people who portrayed themselves to be on a high level both spiritually and intellectually when in fact they were not. This he could not tolerate. The great Kabbalists aspired to ensure that their inside was in sync with their outside, and they termed such a person a *penimi,* literally meaning an "inner person."

Based on what we have discussed in this chapter, the importance of being someone whose inner and outer personas are in sync should now be obvious. We sometimes portray ourselves as happy and positive when we are not. We often even fool ourselves into thinking that we are feeling positive on the inside. But in the end we are sending off negative energy. The main thing here is not about how we act outside, but rather how we think and feel inside. In actuality we often can feel very happy and positive inside and appear melancholy on the outside. Think about a time when you were in the midst of intense work that was going well. Your face would have portrayed seriousness and intensity that could be interpreted as melancholy, but inside you would have been feeling something resembling happiness.

There is, however, one redeeming aspect to acting positive when you feel miserable and that is this aphorism: fake it until you make it. In other words, if you act happy and positive, eventually you will actually feel that way. So it is better to fake feeling happy and positive even if you feel negative. Your goal, then, becomes matching your inner feeling to your outward appearance of happiness and contentment. If your inner and outer personas are in sync, the energy they attract will also be consistent and you can more easily attract what you want from the Divine energy of the universe.

The Hoffman Agency: Uncovering the Genuine

When Lou Hoffman decided to leave one of the major public relations firms in 1986 to start his own boutique company, he had a good idea of what he wanted to do differently. "The problem I was trying to solve was turnover, in clients as well as employees," the fifty-two-year-old California native said. Technology companies tend to drop their PR firms every few months and pick up a new one. As a result, the firms often went strictly for the quick contract and avoided offering advice that wasn't going to result in immediate revenue for the technology company. On the employee side, the female-dominated industry saw employees treated like temp workers because of frequent maternity leaves.

So Hoffman started his own company. He sent out a multipage flier with a picture of a medical bag on the front and the words "He could have been a doctor!" The next page showed a briefcase above the statement "He could have been a lawyer!" On the next page was a picture of Hoffman's scowling mom with her arms akimbo (looking very Jewish-motherish) and the words: "But, no. He got mixed up in this marketing and communications business. And now he's starting his own agency."

Either it was his mother's modeling or his reputation as a PR wizard, but soon the Hoffman Agency had a handful of clients. Hoffman offered them much more than the traditional agency. He promised to stay with them for the life of the firm, to grow with them, and to tailor his services for the long-term growth of the company, not for the quick buck. But he also required loyalty from his clients—he wanted a deep business relationship, not a simple trade of skills for money.

As a result, the Hoffman Agency is a thriving firm today. With hundreds of clients and more than $10 million a year in revenue (along with eight international offices), Hoffman celebrated the twentieth anniversary of his company in 2007, along with many of the original employees and clients who helped him start the firm—and are still involved with it.

Along the way, Hoffman lured many talented PR professionals to work for him. At first it wasn't hard to do because the maternity leave benefits he offered were far more generous than any competitor. Today it's common practice in the industry to provide ample benefits for new mothers as a way of attracting talent, Hoffman can be credited for making a lot of working mothers' lives easier.

A job at the Hoffman Agency is now a much-treasured goal of many PR agents. The firm is renowned for its family atmosphere and the excellent service it provides clients. But that hasn't made hiring any easier. Now he spends much of his time in job interviews trying to ensure that he chooses the right people. And over the years, he's developed a system that would make Rabban Gamliel proud. "Everyone is cheerful and upbeat and excited in a job interview. The problem," Hoffman says, "is that not everyone is going to keep that excitement after a few weeks on the job. The goal of my job interviews is to determine what is genuine about the person. What's on the inside is far more important than what's on the outside."

Hoffman doesn't see much irony in the fact that he's looking for internal authenticity in someone he's hiring to do public relations— the stereotype of which is an overfriendly salesperson with a toothy smile and forced cheerfulness. The real professionals in the business, he points out, are the people who have a true enthusiasm for the client. "I look for people who are as real on the inside as they appear to be on the outside."

Hoffman's quest for such souls begins in the reference stage. Instead of relying on a reference list of superiors given by the potential employee, he does some snooping to find someone who has worked directly with the person, preferably as a subordinate. "If you find the person that sits in the next desk and works with the person day in and day out, you'll find someone who has gotten to know the real person—and that's invaluable."

Next comes interview day, where Hoffman breaks out his secret weapon: his receptionist. He's trained her to engage the candidate in small talk, and then consults her later to find out how the person treated her. As Hoffman says, "We have no hierarchy here and everyone is considered an equal. If the person treats our receptionist snootily because he considers her below himself, he's not the right fit for our company."

During the interview itself, Hoffman will lead the candidate on a winding road of a conversation, mostly consisting of rapid-fire questions. "I'm looking to get a bite on something that really excites the person, maybe a hobby or a sports team or a musician. Then I reel them in and talk about that subject for a long time with them. When you hit on the right subject matter and you see the person getting bright-eyed and passionate, they'll start revealing their genuine selves. The masks come off and you start to get a good handle on who you are dealing with."

Hoffman recalls one candidate who had just finished her career as a television anchorwoman. She wanted to get into public relations at the top. "Everything she said was perfect. Her answers were perfect. Her diction was perfect," he says. But after hours of interviewing her, he hadn't witnessed any passion. If it sounds like it comes from a can, he says, it's not very valuable to his clients.

In a 2007 *Harvard Business Review* article entitled "Maximizing Your Return on People," Laurie Bassi and Daniel McMurrer wrote: "Too many executives still regard—and manage—employees as costs. That's dangerous because, for many companies, people are the only source of long-term competitive advantage. Companies that fail to invest in employees jeopardize their own success and even survival." Many entrepreneurs do not realize that the strength of any organization or enterprise is their employees, but Hoffman did. And the strategy he used to gain employees that would be best for his organization was sound—he wanted to ensure that they were the same inside and out. Hoffman's strategy had an added advantage—by ensuring that his staff was composed of truly positive people both on the outside and on the inside, he was attracting an immense amount of positive energy to his company. And, not surprisingly, while his choice of career may have disappointed his mother at first, things turned out well in the long run. The growth and success of his business exceeded all his expectations.

> INSIGHT FOR BUSINESS: *When you're looking to hire an employee or find a business partner, strive to find a person who has a synergy between their outside appearance and demeanor and what they really feel on the inside. This synthesis of inner and outer will have a positive effect on your business both because of the positive energy it attracts and because it is always a pleasure to work with people who are genuine.*

> INSIGHT FOR LIFE: *Trying to be an actor in real life is a route to nowhere. Strive to be the same person on the outside that you are on the inside. At the same time, set a goal to be positive in all aspects of who you are.*

Meditation

Contemplate the fact that there is more to the universe than the outer veneer of existence that we see. Meditate on the idea that there is a deeper Divine energy that animates all existence. Allow this to sink in deeply. Now recognize that your thoughts can tap directly into the Divine energy and attract the things you want into your life. While meditating on this, think about the types of language and thoughts you are used to thinking and using. Are they mostly positive or negative? Are you happy with your lot or are you unhappy? Are you grateful? Are you optimistic? Isolate the areas you are pessimistic about and analyze whether they are seeing success or not. Notice the connection between the things you are negative about and the things you are not experiencing success in. As you connect deeply with this reality, you will feel intense motivation to both think and talk positively.

CHAPTER 9

THE WAY OF THE WISE

Finding the Right Balance of Character Traits to Succeed in Business

He should not let loose the reins of anger, nor let passion gain mastery over him.

—MAIMONIDES, *GUIDE FOR THE PERPLEXED*

IN CHAPTER 2 WE TALKED ABOUT FINDING OUR AUTHENTIC WILL and desire, and how when we do, motivation flows forth. This, however, must not be confused with following our impulses. One of the biggest challenges people encounter is overcoming emotional urges that lead them down destructive paths. When confronted by potentially destructive temptations, we may become gripped by inappropriate feelings of affection or lust. When wronged, we may experience an intense desire to seek revenge. When encountering another's success, we may feel intense jealousy. And when we get angry, we may feel the urge to strike out. Although the urge to act on an emotion is strong, it is often not the best course of action to take. As was asked (and answered) in Ethics of the Fathers (4:1), "Who is strong? The person who conquers his impulses." This is as true in business as it is in life. When faced with inventory that seems to be selling slowly, we might feel scared of losing money, which might in turn cause us to make a rash and unwise decision. Or when a competitor opens a shop close by, we might feel antagonistic. Following the purely emotional reaction is never the best route to take.

According to the Talmud, every human being is constantly struggling between two competing forces. There is what is known as the *yetzer ha'tov* (the positive inclination) and the *yetzer ha'ra* (the negative inclination). The positive inclination is mainly guided by the intellect and the negative inclination is directed almost entirely by emotional impulses. Think back to any major dilemma you have experienced. Did you feel an emotional tug one way and an intellectual pull the other? Very often, when you analyze the two sides of a dilemma, you can divide them that way: emotions versus intellect.

People often don't recognize the clash between emotions and intellect within themselves. Frequently, what we want to do is not what makes the most sense to do. The great Jewish philosophers have often defined free choice as the ability to choose between an intellectual compulsion and an emotional urge. This applies equally to every aspect of life. Our emotions may tell us to act in a manner that would be ruinous for our business or family life. Our intellect can stop us from acting in a manner that is either personally or financially destructive. One of the keys to success is the ability to strike the right balance between emotional impulses and intellectual persuasion.

Learning How to Balance by Emulating God

The Torah contains great wisdom that helps us balance the intellectual and emotional urges within us. It demands that our actions be informed by a combination of emotion and intellect. The Torah then gives us the greatest teacher ever to show us how—none other than God Himself.

The Torah (Deuteronomy 28:9) says that humans should walk in God's ways. The Talmud (Sotah 14a) explains this in the following way: "As God clothes the naked, as it is written (Genesis 3:21): *And the Lord God made for Adam and for his wife coats of skin, and clothed them*, so too should you clothe the naked. As God visited the sick, as it is written (Genesis 18:3): *And the Lord appeared to him [Abraham] by the oaks of Mamre*, so too should you visit the sick. As God comforted mourners, as it is written (Genesis 25:11): *And it happened after the death of Abraham, that God blessed Isaac his son*, so too should you comfort mourners. As God buried the dead, as it is written (Deuteronomy 34:6): *And He buried him [Moses] in the valley*, so too should you bury the dead."

Maimonides sees this as an independent Torah precept (also known as a mitzvah), and explains that humans are commanded to emulate God to the best of their abilities. This means that we are obliged to imitate the good deeds and lofty attributes by which God is metaphorically described. We must learn from the beautiful, merciful, and kind ways of God, and we are commanded to imitate them. However, there is more to it than that. Inherent in this commandment is useful wisdom for business and management.

But first, let us understand what imitating God means. This is a difficult concept mainly because it's impossible for us to know how God works. Maimonides (the great Jewish philosopher mentioned in the previous chapter), in his philosophical work known as *The Guide for the Perplexed* (Volume 1, Chapter 54), states that although a human being cannot know God, they *can* know His actions. God, the Torah states, is kind, compassionate, merciful, slow to anger, and truthful. But Maimonides points out that although God acts with compassion, He does not actually feel compassion. This is because God is not human. Humans are moved to act in a compassionate manner because they see a situation that fills them with sympathy, and based on that emotional feeling they act with kindheartedness. Because emotions, by definition, are influenced by external situations and God is all-powerful, He can never moved be by emotions. If God were moved to compassion by a circumstance outside of Himself, for example, it would imply that something other than God is able to effect a transformation in Him. This would mean that something other than God has power over Him. Since a monotheistic God must be all-powerful—with no other existence having power over Him—Maimonides concluded that God has no emotions. This, however, does not preclude God from *acting* with (rather than having a feeling of) compassion, love, anger, or any other act that, in humans, would be a reaction to emotion. The difference is that when God acts with anger or mercy it is because it is the correct action at that particular moment. (When the Kabbalists say that God "has emotions" they mean that God "acts in a manner" that is compassionate, merciful, wrathful, etc.)

The reason God would act with love, for example, is because intellectually, love is warranted. God does not react to an emotion that has been awoken within Him. Rather, God acts in accordance with the particular situation and what, according to the Divine Intellect, is necessary. This does not mean that the action, be it loving, angry, compassionate, or anything else, is not carried out with enthusiasm—it may be. But it is not dictated by an emotion. It is instead informed by intellectual necessity. Maimonides says that any person in a leadership or managerial position must do their utmost to follow God's lead and only act when the intellect necessitates it and never to allow emotions to dictate behavior or a course of action.

Very often people get carried away by emotional responses to situations. They may get angry at their employees, colleagues, or family at times when it is either inappropriate or when showing rage is counterproductive. There are also some people (those "who lack understanding") for whom the Talmud says (Berachot 33a) we are forbidden to have compassion because it will not be to their, or society's, benefit. Just because we feel overwhelming compassion for an individual does not mean that an act of kindness is appropriate. All acts of passion must be tempered by the intellect. Acting purely on emotion is always risky and often leads to bad decisions.

Larry A. Mizel, whom we met in Chapter 6, reiterated this point in an interview for this book. Mizel says that he learned deductive reasoning in law school and applies those principles to business. "I consider the ability to think a key element to how I approach my business decisions. Generally when we act on impulse we are wrong because we are doing it for the wrong reason—we just do it because we feel it is a good idea and it therefore does not end up being well planned, well conceived, and carefully executed," Mizel explained.

Often, businesspeople are faced with the tough decision of whether to fire an underproducing employee. Terminating the employment of an individual often means ending the livelihood of a breadwinner, at least in the short term, and an entire family is adversely affected. In a healthy human being, the emotion dictates that the employee should be treated with compassion and be given additional chances to prove themselves. If the employer is angry with the unproductive employee, that emotion might dictate that they fire the employee without due consideration of their personal situation. The intellect can temper that emotion by ensuring that the best be done for both the business and the employee. If firing the employee is the logical thing to do, then at least it is done in a reasoned manner. If retaining that employee is the proper course to follow, then rational steps can be taken to limit its effect on the business. In other words, compassionate acts can be good. But they should never be directed by emotion alone. Our intellect must play a guiding role as well.

There's another reason for this. We all know people whom we have to tiptoe around because they lose their temper at even the smallest perceived indiscretions. We find that such people act in a similar manner towards everybody—even their close family members are nervous around them. This is because they allow their actions to be dictated directly by their emotions. If they realized how inappropriate this display is, it would be easier for them to get along with others.

Louis B. Kravitz, founder and chairman of Paragon Lines, Inc., an international shipping company, explains how this concept applies to business. Throughout his career, Kravitz has always done his best to ensure that his employees are well taken care of. He says that "One must take care of one's employees as one does one's other assets." This means that whenever an employee had a family or a financial situation that needed help, Lou and his company, in almost every case, would step in and offer assistance. Lou describes this as an act of compassion dictated by an emotional response to the suffering of another person. He feels that instead of just easing the trouble he can use his resources to help a person relieve his or her burden.

Over the last year Kravitz and his company have suffered because of this. He allowed a bookkeeper to remain on the payroll and work from home after suffering personal troubles. When the end of the year came, he found that a lot of the bookkeeping work had been done improperly, causing significant problems for the firm.

That example notwithstanding, Kravitz still believes in the principle of compassion and flexibility towards employees when they are experiencing times of trouble. He considers it a logical decision as much as an emotional one. He describes the logic in the following way: "The intellect is the counterbalance to compassion. Logic dictates that, most of the time, helping employees in this way will not benefit the company and often it will not even benefit the employee in the long term. One can only provide the tools to change people's behavior or circumstances. It is always up to the individual to take the tools and use them properly. But if we help ten people and it works out well for one of them, then we will have been amply rewarded for all our efforts." So, in Kravitz's words, "We start off with compassion and then see that compassion through an intellectual prism, drawing a conclusion that, while often not the ideal scenario for the company, is the most helpful response for the individual."

The benefits of acting in this manner are obvious. When we act in a compassionate manner towards another person based purely on emotion, we do so because we believe in our heart that what we are doing will help. In reality, of course, this is often not the case. Giving people money or additional opportunities to prove themselves does not always end up helping them. If you are aware of this and think it through properly, you will take the necessary steps to limit your exposure to the fallout if your help backfires and causes the business to suffer.

INSIGHT FOR BUSINESS: *You should never make a business decision based solely on impulse, because most of the time it will end up being a bad decision. You should always think things through fully. Your ability to do this may end up being your best business asset.*

INSIGHT FOR LIFE: *The notion to "follow your heart" often ends with disastrous consequences. If the relationship makes no sense, it should not be entered into even if the heart wants to. You'll get over that person in time, and in time a person you can both love and intellectually feel comfortable with will show up in your life.*

Victor Niederhoffer: Never Bet on Emotion

Victor Niederhoffer is a hedge fund manager who plays the financial markets like a racetrack. He has made fortunes, and lost them—multiple times. He bases his trading style on the same principles that he learned betting on horses during his adolescence in Brighton Beach, New York.

Niederhoffer is known as quite an eccentric on Wall Street. He never reads any newspapers, except for *The National Enquirer* (which he forces his entire staff to read as well so they can discuss the stories during meetings). He never wears shoes while trading. He reads books incessantly—but only the classics. He claims to have never picked up a book that is less than a hundred years old since his college days. He is rarely seen in society except when he dines with railroad hoboes whom he has befriended.

At the heart of Niederhoffer's business strategies is a simple principle: everything is knowable. He comes up with a trading theory and then tests it against historical data. If the tests show that the concept works, he'll try it in the real markets. He is a master of statistical mathematics, a guru of correlations, and a wizard of standard deviations.

However, Niederhoffer refuses to allow any sign of emotion in his trading office during trading hours. If a staffer cracks a joke and causes someone to laugh, he reminds them of his ban. If there is any physical sign of fear (a trembling voice, a bead of sweat on the brow) on any of his traders, he forces them to take a break and calm down. Trading securities, he believes, must be an entirely intellectual exercise.

According to a passage in his book *The Education of a Speculator* (Wiley, 1998), this concept comes not from the halls of economics departments in universities, but from a childhood observing bettors at a racetrack near his Brooklyn home. The stands are filled with people shouting and screaming as the horses zoom by, their veins popping and their hats flying. These are the people, Niederhoffer realized, who provide the money for the winners. The winners, he noted, are the ones sitting in their seats, watching the race as if they were watching a cloud in the sky. He refers to the character trait that such a winner needs as an "Iron Ass"—a derriere so heavy (and a force of mind to be objective that is just as weighty), that no matter how much emotion and raucousness is going on around them, they don't budge from their position.

Niederhoffer sees this attribute to be just as necessary for success in the financial markets. He writes in his book about the money manager who sells because of panic when the market plummets "after mentally adding on car payments, mortgages, and orthodontist bills." The financial decision, he says, has to be completely removed from any emotion, be it fear, jealousy, anger, etc. He relates his ability to take risks in the market, many of which pay off handsomely, to the fact that he is completely emotionally detached from the meaning of the money. To him, it's merely a method of keeping score. For those who let their emotions run wild while trading securities he has only disdain: "One thing is sure," he writes in his book. "Among the emotionally charged, you will not find one single long-term winner."

Niederhoffer has made billions of dollars in the market. No doubt his ability to detach his decision-making from his emotional impulses has played a large role in that.

INSIGHT FOR BUSINESS: *Decisions must be made in all businesses. Keep in mind that your emotions will always play a part in your business decisions. Being aware of where the two sides in any quandary stem from—either emotion or intellect—will give you more clarity and help make the decision-making process easier.*

INSIGHT FOR LIFE: *You are influenced by two internal forces: the inclination for good and the inclination to act in a destructive manner. When faced with a moral dilemma, you can identify which side is more positive and which is more destructive by tracing them back to either the intellect or the emotion.*

The Middle Path Between Extremes

When our emotional impulses are regulated by our intellect, we are able to easily follow what the great philosopher Maimonides called "the ideal middle path" and navigate between extremes of behavior. To get a proper perspective on what the middle path is and how it benefits every aspect of our business and personal lives, let's sample what Maimonides describes in his book of Torah law known as *Mishnah Torah*.

Maimonides begins by describing different distinct personality types. First he describes the bad-tempered person who is easily angered and always seems agitated and annoyed. Then he describes the opposite type of person who never gets angry and is always placid. He goes on to describe the prideful personality and its opposite, the person who is submissive and always compliant. Maimonides describes the ungrateful person and his or her counterpart, the person who is always appreciative even for the smallest thing and has no real desires or ambitions. Then there is the person who is extremely stingy, not spending a penny even on himself or herself. Their opposite number is the spendthrift. Maimonides notes that other personality traits, such as decency, cruelty, mercy, cowardice, courage, and so on, also follow these models of extremes.

Quoting the ancient Jewish sages, Maimonides says that the right way is to follow the intermediate characteristics of each trait. In other words, one should adopt the characteristic and trait that is midway between the extremes. Maimonides states examples of character traits where this is vital. His first example is most important for all business and personal situations: when is it good for an individual to get angry? Obviously, a bad-tempered person who gets furious over small things is far from ideal. However, when the situation warrants it, or to make a point so that a particular action is not repeated, it is important to display anger. This point is incredibly important. If we get angry often, the anger loses its effect even at a time when anger is warranted. However, if we use anger sparingly, it will have the desired effect every time it is used. Any person who runs a business and manages others must learn this lesson well.

Maimonides also talks about giving to charity, stating that we should not be stingy nor should we be so philanthropic so we have nothing left—we need enough money to survive. This prototype can be used for every characteristic and trait—the middle path should always be followed, avoiding extremes on either side.

The intermediate way is called "the way of the wise" according to Maimonides. The reason for this should now be clear. The wise person always filters his or her emotional urges through their intellect. People who are always angry or are always ungrateful obviously don't think through their reactions before acting. Those who can temper their behaviors and decisions so that they only get angry or show ingratitude at the appropriate time are using their intellect to navigate to a successful end. These people deserve to be called wise.

This is a very important lesson. In addition to calling it "the way of the wise," Maimonides calls the middle path between the two extremes "the way of the Lord." According to tradition, Abraham taught his sons the middle path and expected them to follow it, as the Torah states (Genesis 18:19), "For I know him, that he will command his children and his household after him, and they shall keep *the way of the Lord*, to do justice and judgment." The Torah also states that those who go in this way will reach success: ". . . that the Lord may bring upon Abraham [who went in God's way] all that [the blessings] He said He would do for him."

Clearly, the middle path between passion and cold intellect is what a competent businessperson should follow. As Atticus Capital vice chairman and partner David Slager, whom we met in Chapter 6, says, "You need a lot of passion for an investment. If you see a great investment opportunity and you are just intellectually curious about it, you will not pursue it with the same alacrity as if you are emotionally involved in it as well." However, Slager warns that the investment must primarily make intellectual sense. When the passion for an investment is filtered properly through the intellect, a good investment decision can be made.

The same is true for any other business venture. A person can get very excited and passionate about a new business or career idea. However, excitement and passion alone could be disastrous if the idea makes no financial or business sense. But when the passion is processed through the intellect, the foundation for success has been laid.

INSIGHT FOR BUSINESS: *Your businesses should always straddle the middle path between emotion and intellect. In addition, you should make sure that your business is well balanced in every other area as well. As entrepreneurs, you should make sure that your time is well balanced between maintaining old customers and gaining new ones. The concept of the middle path and balance is applicable to every aspect of your business.*

INSIGHT FOR LIFE: *Anger is one the most important traits to keep in balance. You should only get angry when it is strictly necessary for making a vital point or stand on an issue. Anger loses its effectiveness if overused.*

Don't Stop the Carnival—the Rest of the Story

Herman Wouk's 1965 bestselling novel *Don't Stop the Carnival* is about a New York City businessman who leaves a fast-paced Manhattan life to run a hotel on a small Caribbean island. Things don't go that well for the new hotelier and he never seems to succeed with the hotel.

In a later edition, Wouk states in the forward that the story is actually based on true events and that the hotel was in St. Thomas in the U.S. Virgin Islands, where he once owned a hotel. In the novel, the main character loses all his savings and ends up losing the hotel—which, in fact, happened in real life to Herman Wouk.

Yoni Cohen (not his real name—the real person asked to remain anonymous), an Israeli real estate entrepreneur who was interviewed for this book, was on vacation with his wife in Florida in the early 1970s when he walked past the local courthouse. The sign outside said that they were going to auction a hotel in St. Thomas in the U.S. Virgin Islands at 11 A.M. on the steps of the courthouse. In many states in the United States, it is customary for foreclosed properties to be auctioned in such a manner. As a real estate investor, he thought that observing such an old-fashioned event would be entertaining and that he might even get a good deal on a hotel at the same time, so he decided to come back later that morning for the auction. Upon arriving at the steps of the courthouse, he saw that he was the only person who had shown up for the auction. A judge walked out and invited him inside. The judge sat down and asked him for his opening bid. Cohen bid $100,000 for the property and the judge then countered with a bid for $200,000. "Who am I bidding against?" asked Cohen. "The outstanding mortgage on the property," answered the judge. "And how much is that?" Cohen countered. "$1.7 million," replied the judge. "Well, I will bid $1.8 million" Cohen said and with that he had just bought a hotel.

When he arrived back at the place he was staying, Cohen called his office in New York City and asked them to look up on the map for St. Thomas in the U.S. Virgin Islands. "Why do you want to know?" asked his assistant. "Because we just bought a 200-bedroom hotel there," Cohen answered.

Cohen began spending weekends at his new hotel trying to make it successful. About two months after he bought the hotel a visitor arrived and gave him a copy of Wouk's *Don't Stop the Carnival,* informing him that the book was based on a true story and the failed hotel that was featured in it was the one he had purchased and was now running. This made him even more resolved to turn the hotel around and he decided that he could beat the odds and make the hotel a success. This was not to be. Even though Cohen was beginning to attract tourists to his hotel, the weather ensured that that success would be short lived. St. Thomas was prone to extreme weather conditions and was hit by hurricanes numerous times—the first one destroyed the hotel completely. Unfortunately for Cohen, he couldn't recoup the money to cover the damages because the insurance company that was prepared to insure his hotel went bankrupt as well. He ended up losing his entire $1.8 million investment.

Cohen, who has since been phenomenally successful making real estate deals all over the world, says that he learned two invaluable lessons from his Virgin Islands hotel debacle. "I learned never to make a purchase on emotional impulse. Nowadays, even if I see an investment which seems like an extremely good deal and is very attractive—I resist until I ensure that all the due diligence is done and that the deal makes sense." Cohen talks about the need to avoid the emotional aspect of a business deal. "The deal has to make intellectual sense for me to follow it no matter how much I am attracted to it emotionally," he stated.

However, he learned something else that has helped him tremendously in all his business deals since. "It taught me that when a mistake has been done not to try to repair it for too long, because the energies that are diverted deter me from channeling them into other more productive and profitable projects."

This second lesson that Cohen learned from the hotel failure is also directly related to the emotional/intellectual balance. When we get involved with a project, we often become emotionally attached to it. Because of this, when it fails we continue to try and make it work even though we know intellectually that doing so makes no sense. Our emotional impulses can keep us plugging away at a failing business, spending energy that could be used for a more profitable enterprise. The key is to always temper that emotional impulse, which urges us to continue trying to make it work despite the odds, with a large dose of intellectual common sense.

> **INSIGHT FOR BUSINESS:** *Without an emotional attachment to a business idea or career you will not pursue it with passion. At the same time, however, if the idea or deal has not been properly and methodically thought through, success is likely to be challenging at best. Striking the right balance between the two is vital for success.*

> **INSIGHT FOR LIFE:** *Understand that your emotions can cause you to become attached to relationships that are not working. You should not waste years of your life and tremendous energy in relationships that are failing. Trying to "fix" somebody is never the best alternative no matter how much you love him or her. It's better to spend your energy on a more worthwhile cause that is more likely to succeed.*

The Quantum Leap

The ability to use intellect so that our behavior is always rooted in logic gives us a major advantage over others who just follow their impulses. This is why the Torah says (Deuteronomy 28:9) that humans should walk in God's ways. Maimonides understands this to mean tempering passion with good common sense.

The mystics outline the following difference between angels and humans. Angels were created for a certain purpose and are unable to do anything other than that which they were created to do. Humans, conversely, have ambitions and goals. Humans are always moving. They have choice. There is no such thing as a stationary human being. We are either going forward or backward. A businessperson understands this concept better than anyone. In a business, being stationary means there is no growth. Even if your business is not losing clients or sales, you can be sure that your competitor is moving ahead and becoming better and more effective than you. As your competitors move ahead, in comparison with them you have moved backwards. The same applies to every area of life. Look at it this way: if you could have earned $100 in any given hour and you did not, it is the same as losing $100. There is no such thing as remaining stationary. You either move forward or you regress. As humans, we are charged with the responsibility to constantly move forward from level to level.

But when we walk the middle path or "the way of God" and master our emotions, we are able to move ahead, not in regulated steps that move from one level to the next in a methodical manner, but in a quantum leap. The reason for this, say the mystics, is because it is human nature for the heart to dictate feelings and emotions and therefore compel actions. However, when our actions and emotions are regulated by the intellect, we are transcending our nature and as such we become extraordinary. This gives us a qualitative edge over all others. This is why acting on intellect rather than emotion is described as emulating God.

Often, businesspeople get very excited about a new idea. Have you ever felt compelled to get out of bed to write down a novel idea you had in the middle of the night? The excitement is thrilling and the passion is real. When you are excited about a prospective business opportunity you become emotionally attached to it and intellectual rigor can often take second place. This is the danger zone. If you are to become extremely successful, you must overcome the urge to act immediately and allow your brain to get in gear first.

A Fashion Pioneer Loses All His Money in Phony Business Deal

John (not his real name) was known as a hard-nosed businessman who was almost impossible to fool. Within five years he had built up a large fashion company from nothing, and after making a number of other very large and shrewd investments was able to sell his company and investments for a massive profit. At the age of forty-five John had retired and was living the high life in one of the wealthiest parts of the world. Sometime after he retired, John was befriended by Robert, an apparently honest and pious man whom he had met at the local synagogue. As their friendship progressed, Robert introduced John to a number of new business ventures he was running. Soon enough, Robert was asking John to invest money into his new enterprises. Because of their trusting friendship and the novelty of the business ventures in which Robert was involved, John invested without doing his due diligence. Initially, the returns John was getting on his investments were massive and Robert explained that more money was needed in order to ensure the continued growth of his enterprises. John invested more.

In fact, Robert's enterprises were phony. He was just circulating money to give the impression his businesses were highly profitable. Within a year, the returns stopped coming. Robert was no longer seen in the synagogue and John stopped hearing from him. Not too long afterwards, John received a phone call from his accountant informing him that Robert had declared bankruptcy. However disturbing that news was, what John's accountant said next was even more shattering: "Robert has taken you down with him" John's accountant told him. "You're bankrupt, too."

John admitted that after he went into retirement he let his guard down. "I was in retirement mode," John later said. "He was my friend, he had an exciting idea and I trusted him—I did not check things out properly . . . this was my mistake."

A mistake indeed—it cost John his entire fortune. If only John had allowed his intellect to filter his emotions he would never have invested his entire fortune with one person. If he had thought it through thoroughly, he would have seen through Robert's deception—or at least limited his losses. But John followed his emotions instead. He was taken by Robert's charisma, enthusiasm, and professed religiosity. He was fooled by his own greed when he saw the massive return he was beginning to make on his initial investments. This greed and overexcitement caused him to invest more and more until he was finally fully invested in Robert's schemes. This is when Robert pulled the rug out, leaving John destitute. John had never given his mind the chance to fully get in gear and he suffered terribly as a consequence.

Clearly, the correct balance between emotion and intellect is one of the most important keys to success in business and every other aspect of life as well.

> **INSIGHT FOR BUSINESS:** *Your business can and should be extraordinary. By ensuring that every part of your business is fully filtered through the intellect, you have a considerable advantage over competitors. Most people are guided by emotions—human nature simply acts that way. By being able to rise above that, your business becomes more effective and successful than those of your competitors.*

> **INSIGHT FOR LIFE:** *By not allowing emotion to completely dictate your choice of friends or even life partner, your relationships will be considerably more successful and fulfilling than those who use*

their feelings as the most important barometer of relationship success. Allowing logic and intellect to regulate your relationships creates a quantum leap in their quality and longevity.

Meditation

By learning the techniques of contemplative meditation taught in the Appendix you will become well equipped to overcome emotional urges with intellectual decisions. Spend time learning how to meditate as explained in this book. Use those techniques to contemplate deeply about every decision that you need to make in your business and personal life.

First make sure that you have completely done your research about every detail of the business deal or project. Once this has been achieved, go through the three states of wisdom, understanding, and knowledge discussed in the Appendix, but focus more time and mental energy on the first two stages, ensuring that you have intellectually taken in every detail of the deal at hand. By doing this you will ensure that your intellect has a real influence in every deal, decision, investment, or project your business undertakes—and you will make a quantum leap in your business success.

A Brief Guide to Jewish Meditation

Say the word "meditation" and images of Zen monks in the lotus position probably spring to mind. However, it would be just as historically accurate to envision a pious Jew standing by a tree in a forest, humming to himself. Meditation has a long and thoughtful tradition in Judaism. Much of that tradition was lost in the Holocaust and the forced dispersal of the remaining Eastern European Jews throughout the world.

It has been making a comeback, however. During a time when many Western Jews glanced towards Eastern religions as a means to reconnect with spirituality, some have discovered that a similar meditation-based tradition lies within their own heritage.

Jewish meditation is different from other meditational practices. Other disciplines have the goal of "emptying the mind." Jewish meditation is more concerned with focusing and connecting the mind. It does share in common an important value with other forms of meditation: the real purpose of it is to take control of our thought processes, and therefore our minds.

The Torah recognizes the mind as an incredibly powerful tool. The Kabbalists claim that control of the mind is the key to full control over all aspects of our lives. The method for achieving this is focusing your mind on one particular idea until you are able to connect with it deeply, so deeply that the idea becomes part of who you are. Once this has been achieved, you can act in accordance with that idea in everyday life.

The goal is to take ownership over the idea—to claim it as your own. Often, we will hear or read about an idea and quickly forget about it. On other occasions, we identify with the idea to such an extent that we feel that it is our own. When that happens, the passion we feel for the idea becomes authentic.

Herein lies the difference between how science defines the word "knowledge" and the way the Torah classifies the same word. We can learn something and understand it, but the knowledge won't necessarily have a tangible impact on our lives. Understanding Albert Einstein's theory of relativity does not automatically impact practical aspects of our lives—the idea often remains entirely academic. The Torah, however, defines knowledge differently. The Torah says that Adam "knew" Eve. The word "knew" is famous as a euphemism for cohabitation. But why is "knowing" used regarding Adam and Eve instead of another term—"coming upon"—used elsewhere by the Bible for that act?

The answer is that Adam and Eve had achieved real intimacy with each other. Through the sexual act, they had connected with each other on the deepest level—as the Torah says, they became as one flesh. From the Torah's perspective, knowing something means connecting with it on the deepest level. In the Torah there is a difference between understanding something and having knowledge of it. Understanding an idea means that you are cognitively aware of it. Knowing an idea means that the idea is now a part of you and you identify with it as if it were your own.

So our goal in this book is not only to understand the ideas found here, but rather to actually connect with them to the extent that you feel ownership over the ideas. So when you talk with friends, colleagues, and family about the ideas contained in this book, you should be able to describe them without saying, "I read an interesting idea in a book." You should be able to relate the idea as if it is your own. You should be able to debate and explain the ideas as if you came up with them by yourself. If you feel connected to the ideas of the book to that extent, they will have become a part of who you are. When that occurs, you will operate on their principles without having to consciously force yourself to do so. Contemplative meditation is a tool that will help you to integrate an external idea into your very being. When you contemplate a topic, you connect deeply with it.

Usually, the mind is utilized for understanding things. Contemplative meditation, however, uses the mind to connect with ideas that have already been understood. By contemplating on an already comprehended idea, it permeates the mind to the degree that it filters down and also impacts the emotions. Through contemplation, we can become excited about an idea.

So the goal is to take an idea that you would like to make a part of your life and connect with it on a very deep level. The following will explain how to practice contemplative meditation.

But first a word of encouragement. Please don't get disheartened if this exercise does not work the first time—it takes time to get your mind used to being totally focused in one direction. It is recommended that you begin doing this exercise for two minutes per day and add on fifteen to thirty seconds of meditation each time you perform the meditative exercise (fifteen minutes is a good goal).

Now we are ready to begin. First, find a quiet room where you will not be disturbed for the time you want to meditate. Wherever you decide to practice your meditation, ensure that you are completely relaxed. You may want to focus on your breathing to help yourself relax. Now, decide which chapter of the book you wish to meditate on and implement in your business or life. Accordingly, choose what in your life or business you would like to change. Think about how your current method of working is damaging you or your business and what you would like to replace it with based upon the idea you learned and understood (understanding is key: ensure that you have understood the ideas properly before beginning the meditative process) from the chosen chapter of the book. Use the meditation tips at the end of each chapter as a pointer for the meditation you undertake. Now state the concept you wish to meditate on in three to seven words. For example you might choose the words, "Humility is good for business." (Use the meditation at the end of each chapter to help with this.)

When you become fully relaxed, your mind will begin to roam—random thoughts will enter and attempt to take over the process. As this happens, refocus on the idea—and words—you wish to meditate on. Now keep the phrase in mind. Allow your mind to go over these words again and again. You may mouth them or say these words quietly if you wish.

You are now ready to enter the three stages of meditation. According to the mystics, the three contemplative stages are: 1) *chochmah*—wisdom; 2) *binah*—understanding; and 3) *daat*—knowledge (i.e., connecting).

Stage one: *chochmah*—wisdom. For this, just contemplate the phrase you are repeating. Make sure not to allow any other random thought disturb your focus on the words you have been repeating—you may continue saying the phrase over and over again to help you focus on it. Keep focusing on the phrase—on each word of it and the meaning it has to you. Do not allow any other thought to interrupt. If other thoughts come in, begin to say your phrase a little louder to block them out and concentrate on the words more deeply. Within a couple of minutes this should take you to the next stage.

Stage two: *binah*—understanding. Start to think about all the details that your phrase represents. Now you can utilize other thoughts to augment the contemplative process. If other thoughts enter your mind use them to enhance the concept you are meditating on. So if the thought of a car, for example, enters your mind, use the idea of a car to further your contemplation about the concept from the book. For example, if you are contemplating the idea of humility and a new car enters your mind think about how new cars affect your humility. Based on the concept of humility found in the book, do new cars make you more or less humble? Do this for at least one minute. As you do this you should feel the magnitude of the idea; it will become increasingly clear to you how helpful and wonderful the idea is for you and your business. If this is done correctly you will begin to feel an emotional sense of excitement about the idea. Once a minute is up, you will automatically have entered into stage three.

Stage three: *daat*—connecting. As you continue contemplating the details of the idea, you will begin to feel connected to it. You will feel excited about implementing it in your life and business. You will now begin to feel that this idea is your own. You should now feel very motivated to carry it out and make it a part of your life and how you operate. Allow that feeling of connection with the concept to dwell with you.

Finally, now that you are motivated, remind yourself of the positive thing you would like to achieve or the negative habit that you would like to cease doing. Now think about it using stage one, *chochmah*, or wisdom. Again, to help you anchor the thought in your mind, you may actually mouth it over and over again. You may now go over the process again, this time taking it a step deeper and therefore connecting even more intensely with the idea you would like to incorporate into your business or life. Try to do this each day. Set aside time in your daily schedule for contemplative meditation. It would be a good idea to stick with one idea found in the book for at least a week so that changes are allowed to take hold before others are introduced. This is a powerful tool to ensure positive change in every aspect of life. Good luck.

INDEX

ABOUT THE AUTHORS

RABBI LEVI BRACKMAN is a popular Judaic scholar, writer, and teacher. He has taught on three continents and his weekly articles are read by thousands globally. He also writes a regular column published on Ynetnews.com, the website of the largest Israeli daily newspaper—*The Yedioth Ahronoth.*

His articles have also been published in *The Denver Post* and *The Jewish Chronicle,* as well as in numerous other publications both in print and on the Internet. Levi Brackman is also the founder and director of a number of successful organizations, including Judaism in the Foothills and The Movement for a Tolerant World. Rabbi Brackman's inspirational commentaries can be seen daily on Dish Network's Dreidel TV Channel 9413. He also has an hour-long weekly program on KSBS-TV in Denver. He also runs a coaching and consulting practice for businesspeople and executives seeking greater growth and fulfillment from their businesses and careers. Rabbi Levi Brackman is known for his accessibility and can be contacted through his website: www.levibrackman.com.

SAM JAFFE has more than fifteen years of experience covering, and participating in, the world of high-stakes finance. He has been on the staff of *The Wall Street Journal, SmartMoney* magazine, *Bloomberg Markets* magazine, *BusinessWeek* and *The Scientist* magazine. He has also written articles for numerous publications, including *The New Repub-lic*, *The New York Times*, *Scientific American*, and *Wired* magazine. He runs a successful business consultancy for renewable energy compa-nies and is now in the process of launching a solar energy startup. He comments on business events at his blog at www.gatesofemporia.com. Sam lives with his wife and three children in Evergreen, Colorado.